Name _____

Alphabet Practice

Write the missing uppercase letters or lowercase letters.

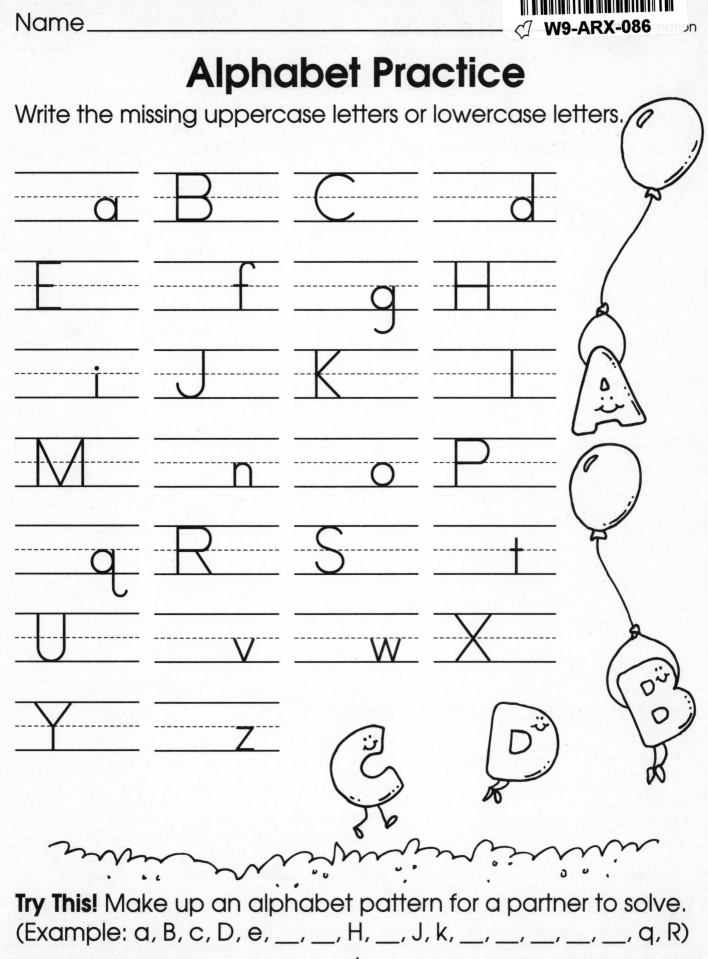

a B C d

E f g H

i J K I

M n o P

q R S t

U v w X

Y z

Try This! Make up an alphabet pattern for a partner to solve.
(Example: a, B, c, D, e, __, __, H, __, J, k, __, __, __, __, __, q, R)

1

Aa, Bb, Cc

Write the alphabet neatly.
Write uppercase letters and lowercase letters.

Try This! Choose a letter you want to practice writing. Write it
five times on the back of this paper. Circle your best one.

2

Starts the Same

Circle the three pictures in each row that begin with the same sound.

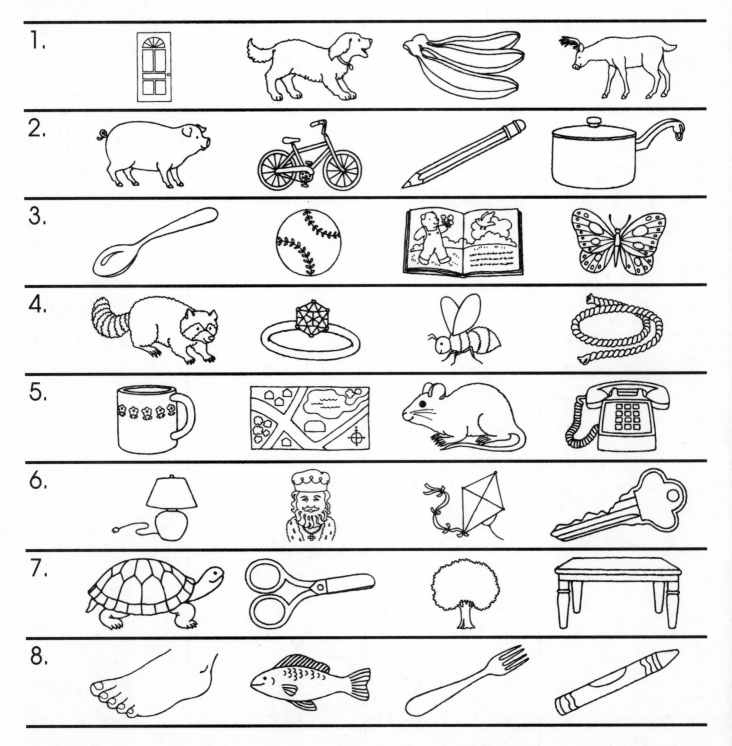

Try This! Pick a row. Draw a new picture for the same sound.

FS-32056 First Grade Review

What Sound Does It Begin With?

Look at the picture. What sound does it begin with?
Fill in the circle next to the matching letter.

Try This! Pick a letter. Name a word that starts with that sound.

4

Fun With Blends

Write the missing blend: **bl**, **cl**, **fl**, **gl**, **pl**, or **sl**.

1. _____ ock

2. _____ obe

3. _____ ag

4. _____ ant

5. _____ ock

6. _____ ue

7. _____ ide

8. _____ ute

9. _____ ower

10. _____ oud

11. _____ anet

12. _____ ed

13. _____ anket

14. _____ own

15. _____ ove

16. _____ ane

Try This! Use **L** blends to write five words that end with **ow**.

Which Blend?

Write the missing blend: **br**, **dr**, **gr**, **pr**, or **tr**.

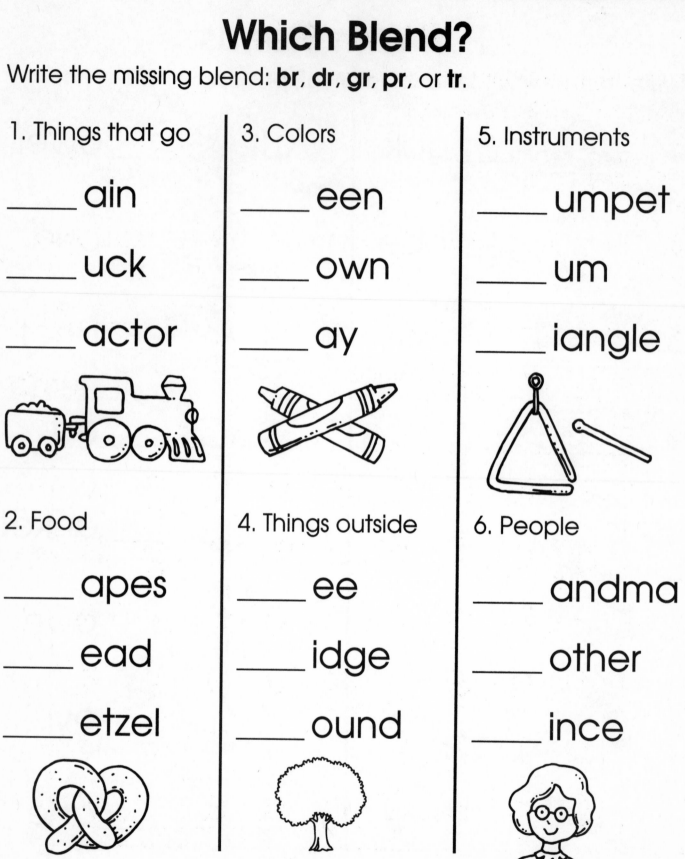

1. Things that go

____ ain

____ uck

____ actor

2. Food

____ apes

____ ead

____ etzel

3. Colors

____ een

____ own

____ ay

4. Things outside

____ ee

____ idge

____ ound

5. Instruments

____ umpet

____ um

____ iangle

6. People

____ andma

____ other

____ ince

Try This! How many words can you write that rhyme with **train**?

FS-32056 First Grade Review

Puzzle Fun

Fill in the blank with **ch**, **sh**, or **th**.
Find and circle each word in the puzzle.

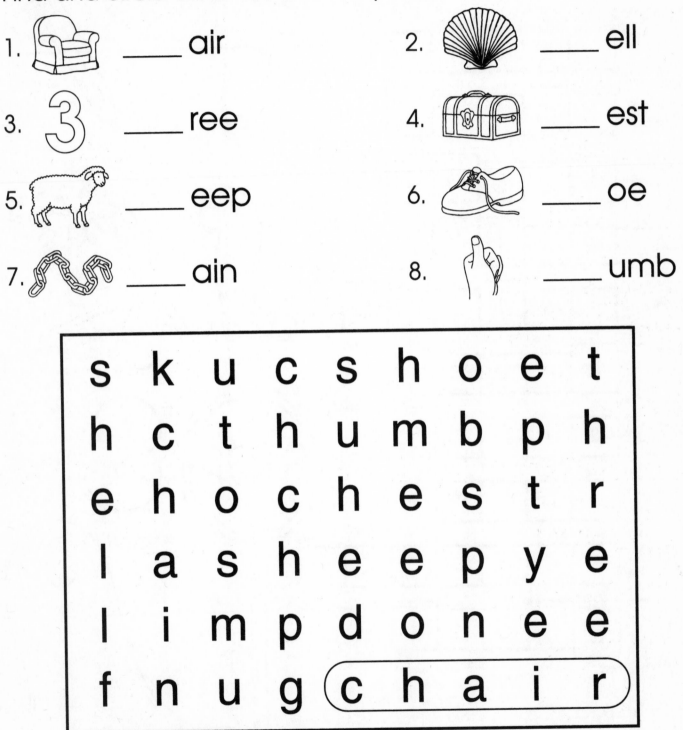

1. ___ air

2. ___ ell

3. ___ ree

4. ___ est

5. ___ eep

6. ___ oe

7. ___ ain

8. ___ umb

```
s  k  u  c  s  h  o  e  t
h  c  t  h  u  m  b  p  h
e  h  o  c  h  e  s  t  r
l  a  s  h  e  e  p  y  e
l  i  m  p  d  o  n  e  e
f  n  u  g  c  h  a  i  r
```

Try This! Write five more words that start with **ch**, **sh**, or **th**.

Name_____

Silent Consonants

These words all have silent consonants.
Color the boxes of the consonants you do not hear.

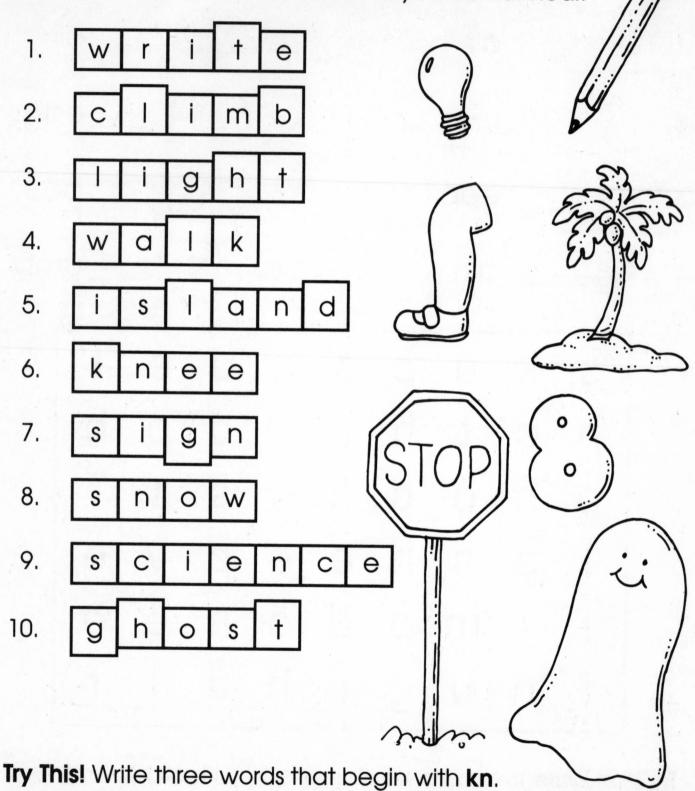

1. w r i t e
2. c l i m b
3. l i g h t
4. w a l k
5. i s l a n d
6. k n e e
7. s i g n
8. s n o w
9. s c i e n c e
10. g h o s t

STOP

Try This! Write three words that begin with **kn**.

Which Vowel?

Write the missing short vowel: **a**, **e**, **i**, **o**, or **u**.

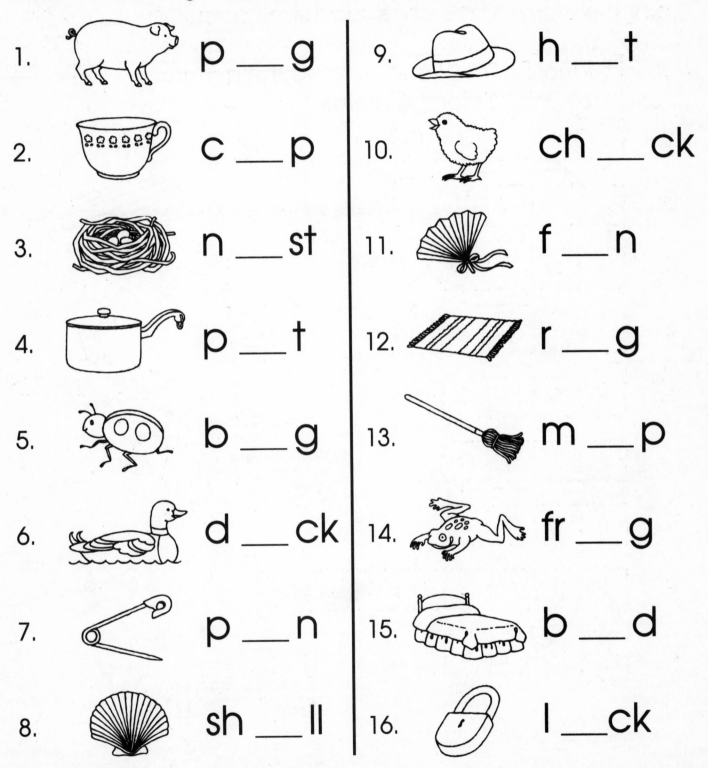

1. p __ g

2. c __ p

3. n __ st

4. p __ t

5. b __ g

6. d __ ck

7. p __ n

8. sh __ ll

9. h __ t

10. ch __ ck

11. f __ n

12. r __ g

13. m __ p

14. fr __ g

15. b __ d

16. l __ ck

Try This! Change the vowel in **b __ g** to make five different words.

FS-32056 First Grade Review

Step by Step

1. Short **a** words: Draw a ○ around the pictures.
2. Short **e** words: Draw an **X** on the pictures.
3. Short **i** words: Draw a □ around the pictures.
4. Short **o** words: Draw a △ around the pictures.
5. Short **u** words: Color the pictures.

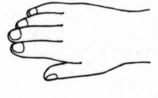

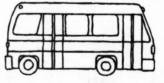

Try This! Circle a short **i** word in this sentence.

10

Silent E Words

Write the missing long vowel **a**, **i**, **o**, or **u** in the first blank. Write the silent **e** in the second blank.

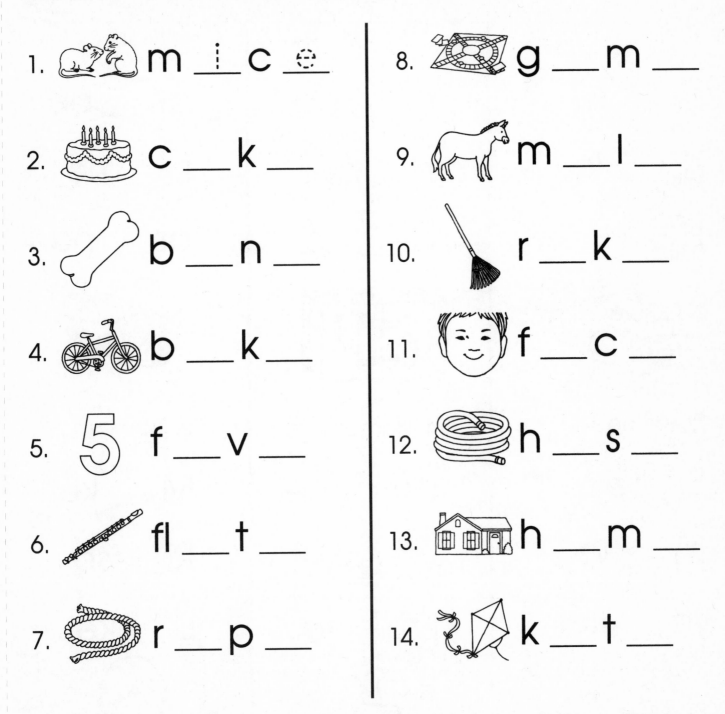

1. m _i_ c _e_

2. c __ k __

3. b __ n __

4. b __ k __

5. f __ v __

6. fl __ t __

7. r __ p __

8. g __ m __

9. m __ l __

10. r __ k __

11. f __ c __

12. h __ s __

13. h __ m __

14. k __ t __

Try This! Add a silent **e** to change a short vowel word to a long vowel word. (Examples: tap—tape, cut—cute)

Name_____

Long Vowels

Write the missing long vowel: **a**, **i**, **o**, or **u**.
Circle the silent **e**.

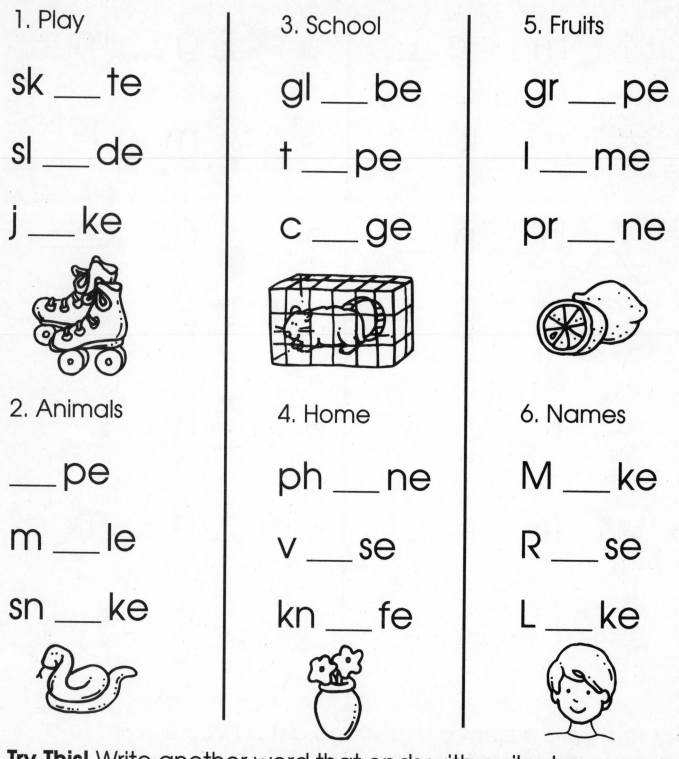

1. Play

sk __ te

sl __ de

j __ ke

2. Animals

__ pe

m __ le

sn __ ke

3. School

gl __ be

t __ pe

c __ ge

4. Home

ph __ ne

v __ se

kn __ fe

5. Fruits

gr __ pe

l __ me

pr __ ne

6. Names

M __ ke

R __ se

L __ ke

Try This! Write another word that ends with a silent **e**.

© Frank Schaffer Publications, Inc.

FS-32056 First Grade Review

It Takes Two

Match each word to its picture.
Underline the two vowels in each word.

1. p<u>ai</u>l

2. boat

3. fruit

4. chain

5. tree

6. sheep

7. train

8. pie

9. goat

10. rain

11. coat

12. soap

13. seal

14. tie

15. stream

16. road

Try This! Make a list of **ee** words. (Example: seed)

13

Name _____

Y Can Be a Vowel

In the word *funny,* the **y** makes the long **e** sound.
In the word *dry,* the **y** makes the long **i** sound.
Say each word. Write it under the correct vowel sound.

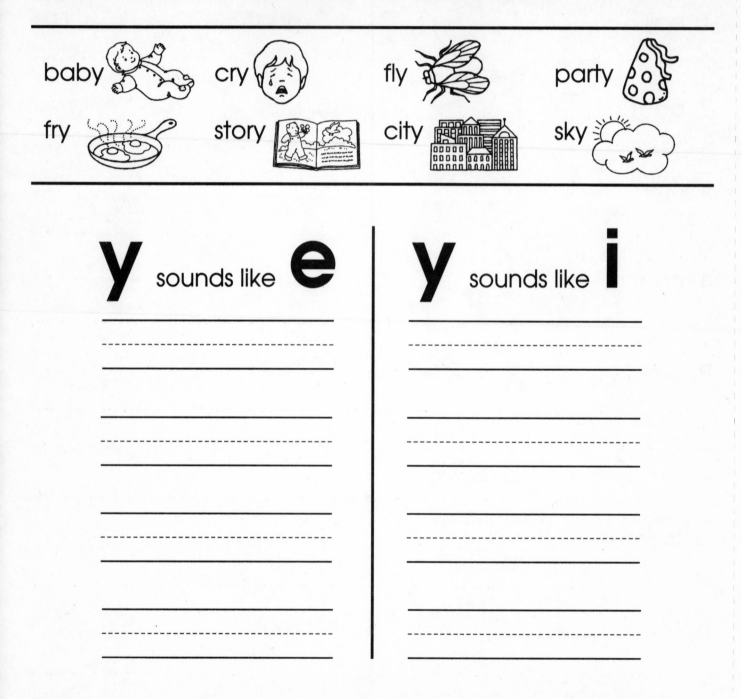

baby   cry   fly   party

fry   story   city   sky

y sounds like **e**

_____

_____

_____

_____

_____

_____

_____

_____

y sounds like **i**

_____

_____

_____

_____

_____

_____

_____

_____

Try This! Think of another word that ends with the letter **y**.
Does it sound like a long **e** or a long **i**?

14

Rhyming Words

Circle the three pictures in each row that rhyme.

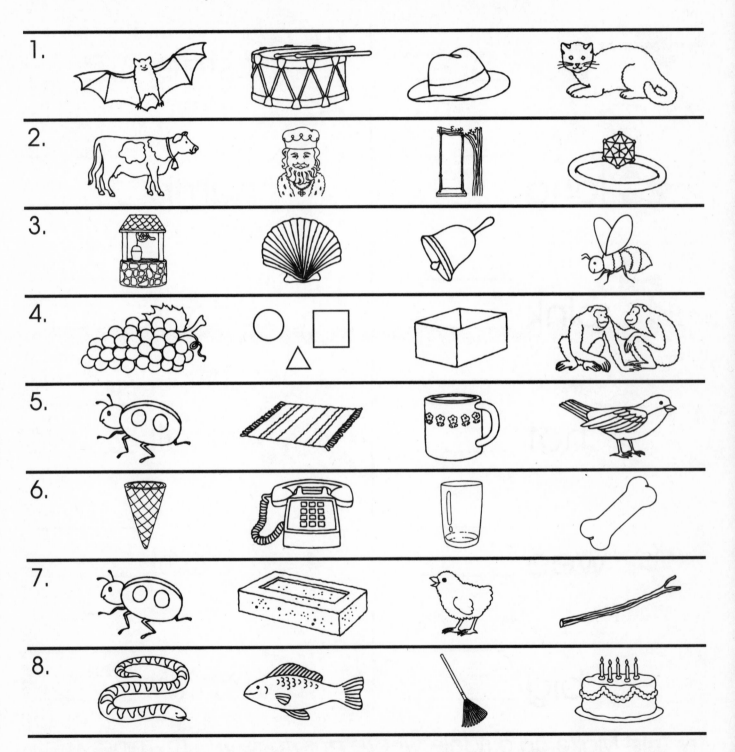

Try This! Choose a row. Think of a new rhyming word.
Draw its picture.

15

Rhyme Time

Write the rhyming word that matches the picture.

1. wet _net_

2. long _____

3. pink _____

4. hot _____

5. wee _____

6. big _____

7. steel _____

8. numb _____

9. bright _____

10. small _____

11. cool _____

12. white _____

Try This! Make up a riddle whose answer is two rhyming words. (Example: What do you call someone who collects bugs? A creeper keeper)

FS-32056 First Grade Review

Name _____

Twins

Write the word from the fishtank that has the same meaning.

large	begin	high	nice
earth	under	noisy	shut

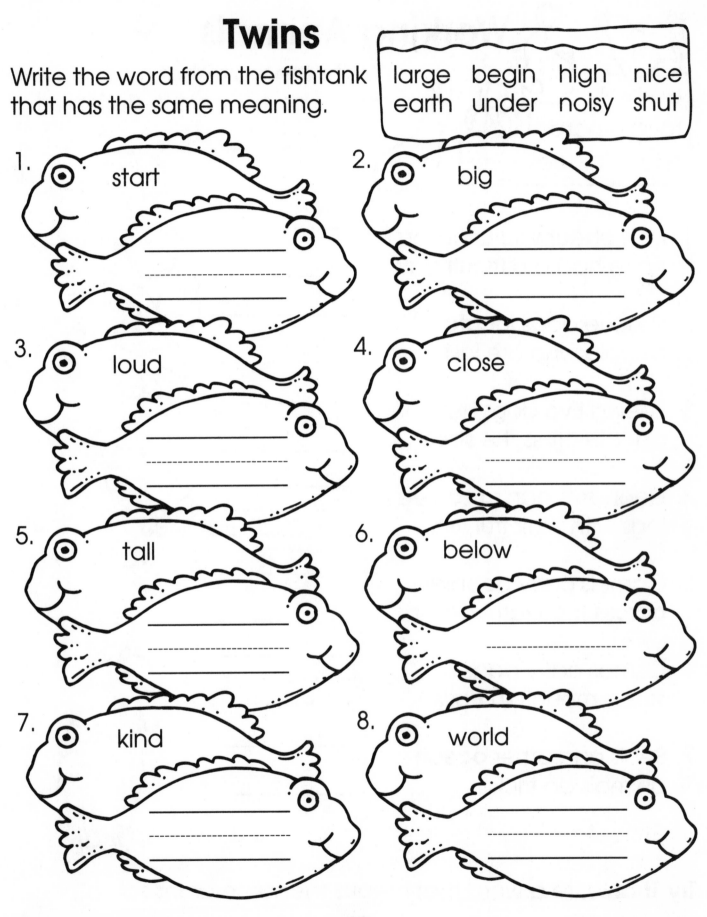

1. start

_____

2. big

_____

3. loud

_____

4. close

_____

5. tall

_____

6. below

_____

7. kind

_____

8. world

_____

FS-32056 First Grade Review

Name _____

Working Animals

Write the word that means the same as the word in **dark** print.

paths	
road	hard
find	lift	sea	over

1. Pets cheer you up if you have had a **difficult** day. _____

2. Rescue dogs **locate** people who are lost. _____

3. Seeing Eye dogs help blind people cross the **street**. _____

4. Elephants can **raise** heavy logs with their trunks. _____

5. Camels carry people **across** the warm desert. _____

6. Llamas carry bags up steep mountain **trails**. _____

7. Seals and other **ocean** animals do tricks. _____

Try This! Write a word that means the same as **insect**.

18 FS-32056 First Grade Review

Name _____ Antonyms

Up and Down

Match each word to its opposite.

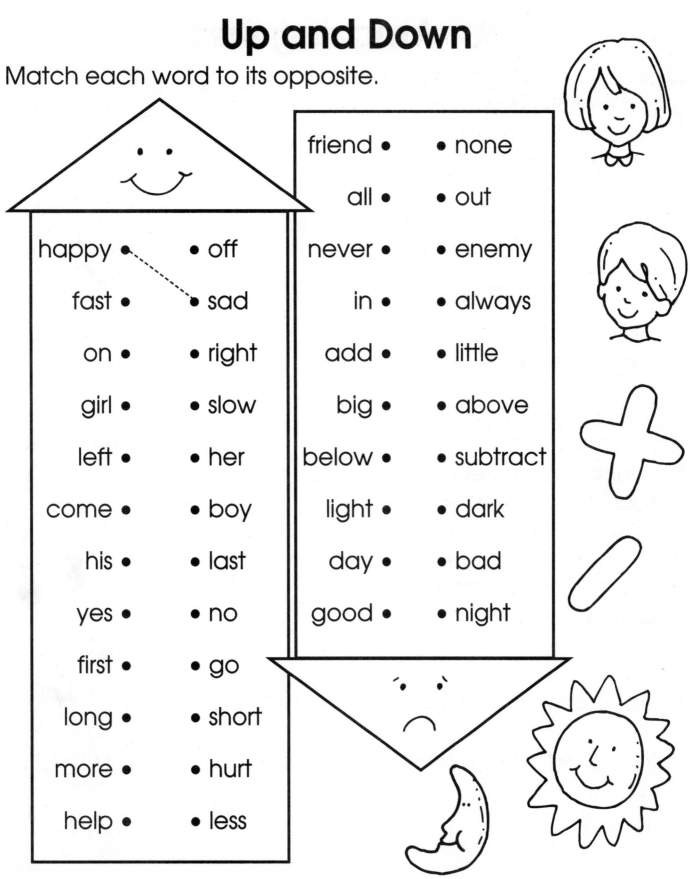

friend • • none
all • • out
never • • enemy
in • • always
add • • little
big • • above
below • • subtract
light • • dark
day • • bad
good • • night

happy • • off
fast • • sad
on • • right
girl • • slow
left • • her
come • • boy
his • • last
yes • • no
first • • go
long • • short
more • • hurt
help • • less

Try This! Write three other opposite word pairs.

© Frank Schaffer Publications, Inc.

FS-32056 First Grade Review

Your Amazing Body

Write the word that is the opposite
of the word in **dark** print.

loud	left
cold	asleep
big	out

1. Your brain tells your body what to do when

   _____

   you are **awake** and _____ .

   _____

2. Your **right** eye and _____ eye see
   different things.

   _____

3. Your ears can hear _____ and **soft**
   sounds.

4. Your skin lets you feel whether things are

   _____

   hot or _____ .

   _____

5. Your body has _____ and **little** bones.

6. Your chest moves when you breathe

   _____

   in and _____ .

Try This! Think of things your hands can do that are opposites.

Animal Words

Use a word from each wing to make one compound word for each picture.

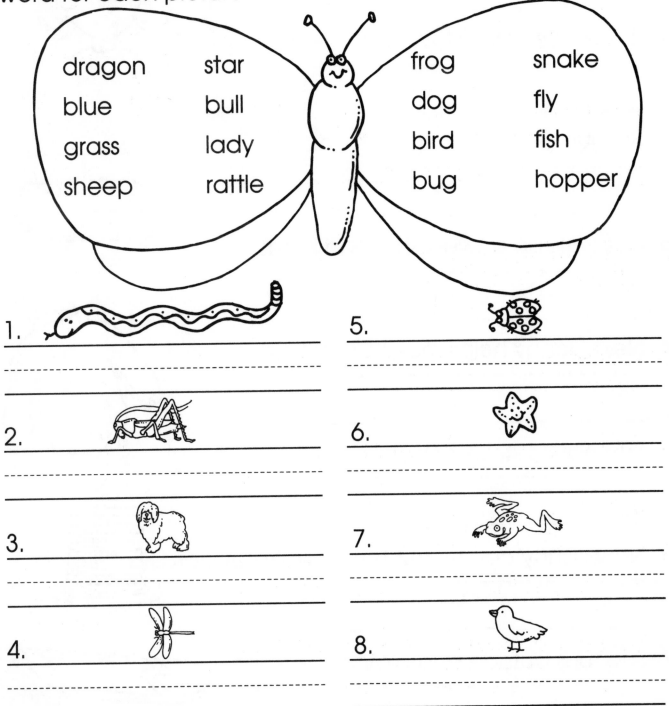

dragon	star
blue	bull
grass	lady
sheep	rattle

frog	snake
dog	fly
bird	fish
bug	hopper

1. _____

2. _____

3. _____

4. _____

5. _____

6. _____

7. _____

8. _____

Try This! See how many compound words you can think of in two minutes. Write them on the back of this paper.

Jenny's Birthday

Circle each compound word.
Write the compound word on the line.

1. It is Jenny's birthday.

   _____

   _ _ _ _ _ _ _ _ _ _ _ _ _ _ _ _

   _____

2. She jumps out of her daybed.

   _____

   _ _ _ _ _ _ _ _ _ _ _ _ _ _ _ _

   _____

3. She puts on a sweatshirt and jeans.

   _____

   _ _ _ _ _ _ _ _ _ _ _ _ _ _ _ _

   _____

4. Next, Jenny helps make breakfast.

   _____

   _ _ _ _ _ _ _ _ _ _ _ _ _ _ _ _

   _____

5. She eats a stack of pancakes.

   _____

   _ _ _ _ _ _ _ _ _ _ _ _ _ _ _ _

   _____

6. Now Jenny can try out her new skateboard.

   _____

   _ _ _ _ _ _ _ _ _ _ _ _ _ _ _ _

   _____

7. She runs outside and plays.

   _____

   _ _ _ _ _ _ _ _ _ _ _ _ _ _ _ _

   _____

Try This! Write a list of things at home that are compound words.

Colorful Robots

1. Color two robots orange. Color eight robots blue.

2. Color six robots brown. Color four robots green.

3. Color nine robots purple. Color one robot yellow.

4. Color three robots black. Color seven robots red.

5. Color five robots blue. Color zero robots green.
Leave five robots white.

Try This! Write your favorite color and number.

FS-32056 First Grade Review

Bunches of Balloons

Color the balloons.

Color five green.
Color four brown.
Leave three white.

Color ten orange.
Color one black.
Color two yellow.

Color six blue.
Color nine red.

Color eight purple.
Color seven brown.

Try This! What colors are you wearing today? Write them.

FS-32056 First Grade Review

Find the Word

Fill in the circle next to the matching word.

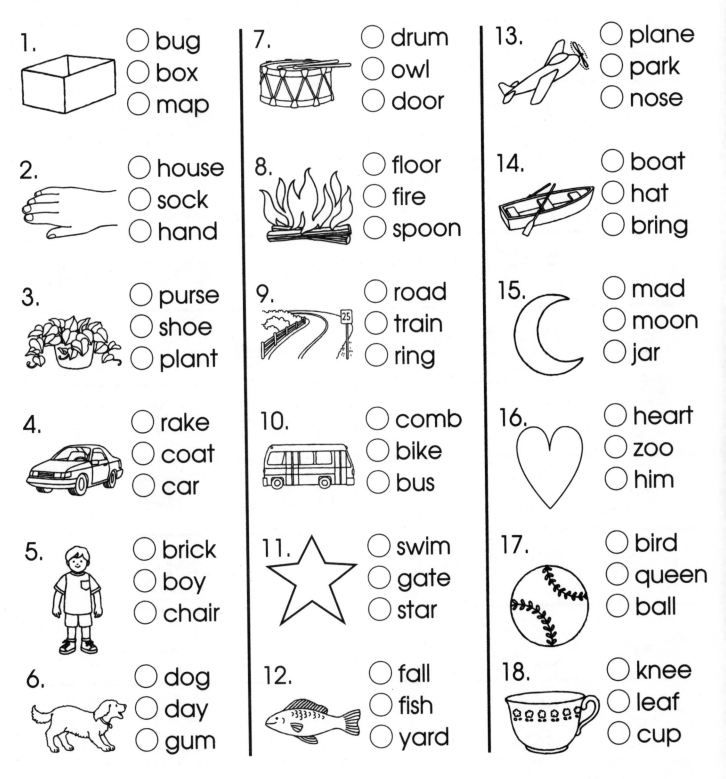

1. ○ bug ○ box ○ map

2. ○ house ○ sock ○ hand

3. ○ purse ○ shoe ○ plant

4. ○ rake ○ coat ○ car

5. ○ brick ○ boy ○ chair

6. ○ dog ○ day ○ gum

7. ○ drum ○ owl ○ door

8. ○ floor ○ fire ○ spoon

9. ○ road ○ train ○ ring

10. ○ comb ○ bike ○ bus

11. ○ swim ○ gate ○ star

12. ○ fall ○ fish ○ yard

13. ○ plane ○ park ○ nose

14. ○ boat ○ hat ○ bring

15. ○ mad ○ moon ○ jar

16. ○ heart ○ zoo ○ him

17. ○ bird ○ queen ○ ball

18. ○ knee ○ leaf ○ cup

Try This! Draw pictures to match these words: **cat, rope, bug.**

Which Picture?

Read the word. Circle the matching picture.

1. tree
2. book
3. sun
4. dog
5. bath
6. two
7. big
8. food
9. eye
10. sea

11. light
12. rock
13. bell
14. wood
15. wheel
16. game
17. brush
18. rain
19. lion
20. snake

Try This! Write the names of four pictures that are not circled.

26

FS-32056 First Grade Review

What Does It Say?

Circle the picture that matches each sentence.

1. The boy reads a book.

2. The cat is in the tree.

3. The duck swims in the pond.

4. The girl is sad.

5. The pigs like to dance.

6. The sun is behind a cloud.

Try This! Write a sentence and draw a picture to match.

27

Sentence Match-up

Draw a line from each sentence to its picture.

The birds are in the nest.

The mouse has a hat.

The boy is on the slide.

The bear waters the plants.

The girl is playing ball.

It is an apple tree.

The children are swinging.

The pine tree has snow on it.

The fish is in a bowl.

The people are in line.

Try This! Draw a picture to match **The bunny drives a car.**

Name _____

Let's Go to School

Write the missing words.
Use words from the box.

walk	school
bus	late
car	ride

1. There are many ways to go to _____.

2. Children who live nearby can _____.

3. If they are _____ , they need to run.

4. Some children ride the _____.

5. Others like to _____ their bikes.

6. Parents can drive them in a _____.

Try This! Draw a picture showing how you go to school.
Write a sentence to match.

FS-32056 First Grade Review

All Kinds of Helpers

Write the missing words.
Use words from the box.

fires	learn
go	safe
teeth	sick

1. A police officer helps people stay _____.

2. A firefighter helps stop _____.

3. A doctor or nurse helps _____ people.

4. A dentist helps people care for their _____.

5. A bus driver helps people _____ places.

6. A teacher helps children _____.

Try This! Write a sentence about another helper.

A Nature Hike

Read the story. Write the answers.

Tina went on a hike.
She looked for leaves.
She listened to birds.
She smelled some flowers.
She felt a smooth rock.

1. Where did Tina go?

_____

_____

2. What did she look for?

_____

_____

3. What did she hear?

_____

_____

4. What did she touch?

_____

_____

5. What did she use her nose for?

_____

_____

6. What would you do on a hike?

_____

_____

Try This! Write something Tina might taste on a hike.

A Fun Trip

Read the story. Write the answers.

Juan is very happy.
He is flying on an airplane.
Juan is going to see his grandma.
She turns 80 years old next week.
Juan will have a fun trip.

1. Whom is Juan going to see?

_____

_____

2. How is he getting there?

_____

_____

3. Who is having a birthday soon?

_____

_____

4. How do you know his grandma lives far away?

_____

_____

5. How does Juan feel about the trip?

_____

_____

6. Where would you like to go on a trip?

_____

_____

Try This! Draw a picture that shows part of the story.

Time for Dinner

Which sentence tells the main idea of the whole picture?
Fill in its circle.

○ A giraffe likes to eat.
○ Trees grow near the giraffe.
○ A giraffe eats leaves.

○ A squirrel eats nuts.
○ A squirrel lives in a tree.
○ A squirrel hides nuts in a tree.

○ Bear cubs play.
○ Mother bear teaches her cubs to hunt for food.
○ Bear cubs drink.

○ A lizard sits on a rock.
○ A lizard catches a bug with its tongue.
○ A bug is on a rock.

Try This! Draw a picture to match this main idea: **Different people like different foods.**

Summer Fun

Which sentence tells the main idea of the whole picture?
Fill in its circle.

○ The children are selling lemonade.
○ The children made lemonade.
○ The children are outside.

○ Ken likes the pool.
○ Ken likes swimming in the pool.
○ The pool is full of water.

○ Nan has a sister.
○ Nan is playing.
○ Nan and her sister play together.

○ Brad is sleeping.
○ Brad is picking flowers.
○ Flowers need to be watered.

Try This! Draw a picture showing what you like to do in the summer. Write a sentence about it.

Family Time

Fill in the circle of the sentence that tells the main idea of the story.

Tony likes to help his mom cook.
They make a lot of pasta.
Then they eat a lot of pasta.
Cooking with his mom is fun.

○ Tony loves his mom.
○ Tony likes the food his mom cooks.
○ Tony likes to cook with his mom.

Michelle's dad is teaching her to speak French.
She can say *hello* and *goodbye*.
She can count to 10.
She can say *please* and *thank you*.

○ Michelle can count to 10 in French.
○ Michelle's dad is teaching her French.
○ French is like English.

Try This! Draw a picture showing what you like to do with someone in your family. Write a sentence about it.

35

Fun With Science

Fill in the circle of the sentence that tells the main idea of the story.

Ashley has a new magnet.
She is finding out what things will stick to it.
She puts it near her pencil.
Nothing happens.
She puts it near a paper clip.
The paper clip sticks to the magnet.

○ Paper clips stick to magnets.
○ Ashley is learning what sticks to magnets.
○ Ashley has a magnet.

The sun is very important to us.
The sun gives off heat.
The sun's heat keeps us warm.
We get light from the sun.

○ The sun is a star.
○ The sun is very important.
○ We get heat from the sun.

Try This! Write sentences about the sun. Can you think of the main idea of your sentences?

What's on the Cover?

Look at the book's cover to answer the questions.

What is the title of the book?

_____

Who is the author of the book?

_____

Who is the illustrator of the book?

_____

Try This! Design your own book cover.

A New Cover

Read a book. Make a new cover for the book.
Write the title, the author, and the illustrator.
Draw a picture of your favorite part.

Title
_____
- -
_____
_____
- -
_____

Author
_____
- -

Illustrator
_____
- -
_____

Try This! Look at the cover of two books. How are they alike and different?

FS-32056 First Grade Review

Name _____

Beginning, Middle, End

Read a story. Draw pictures that show what happened at the beginning, in the middle, and at the end.

Beginning

Middle

End

Title _____

_____

Try This! Show and explain your pictures to a partner.

What Happened?

Read a book. Finish the sentences.

I read the book
_____
- -
_____

At the beginning of the story
_____
- -
_____
- -
_____

In the middle of the story
_____
- -
_____
- -
_____

At the end of the story
_____
- -
_____
- -
_____

Try This! Draw a picture of your favorite part of the story.

My Favorite Character

Think of your favorite book. Draw and label a picture of your favorite character from the book. Then finish the sentence.

Character

_____

- -

_____

I liked this character the best because _____

- -

_____

- -

_____

- -

_____

- -

_____

Try This! Write three ways you and the character are alike.

FS-32056 First Grade Review

An Important Character

Think of your favorite story. Draw the most important character from the story. Answer the questions.

1. What is the character's name?

_____
- -
_____

2. What are three words that describe him or her?

_____
- -
_____

3. Why do you think this character is the most important?

_____
- -
_____
- -
_____
- -
_____

Try This! If you were acting out the story, which character would you want to be? Write why.

42   FS-32056 First Grade Review

Reality or Fantasy?

Some stories are realistic. This means that the story could happen in real life.

Some stories are fantasy. This means the story could not happen in real life.

Read the sentences. Color the present red if it could really happen. Color the present green if it could not happen.

A dog is riding a bike.

The rock is magic.

Eggs come from a chicken.

The cat played with the yarn.

The pig put on his shirt.

The bird built a nest.

Nan went fishing.

The boy rode in a plane.

A fish went to the movies.

The frog drives the bus.

The girl can fly.

The bear ate the fish.

Try This! Draw a picture of a fantasy.

Could It Really Happen?

Some stories are realistic. This means that the story could happen in real life.

Some stories are fantasy. This means the story could not happen in real life.

Read each sentence below. Color the scoop of ice cream blue if it could really happen. Color the scoop of ice cream yellow if it could not happen.

Try This! Write three examples of things that could happen.

44

At the Circus

Write each set of words in ABC order.

1.
lion
horse
elephant

2.
tie
hat
wig

3.
ticket
tent
trapeze

4.
bear
bicycle
balloon

5.
clown
circus
children

6.
peanuts
popcorn
program

Try This! Think of five funny clown names. Write them in ABC order.

FS-32056 First Grade Review

Fun at the Park

Write **1**, **2**, and **3** in the circles to put the words in ABC order.

A. ◯ trees
    ◯ grass
    ◯ flowers

B. ◯ ducks
    ◯ fish
    ◯ pond

C. ◯ stream
    ◯ waterfall
    ◯ rocks

D. ◯ kite
    ◯ ball
    ◯ jump rope

E. ◯ skates
    ◯ wheelchair
    ◯ scooter

F. ◯ dogs
    ◯ bugs
    ◯ birds

G. ◯ sand
    ◯ pail
    ◯ shovel

H. ◯ seesaw
    ◯ swings
    ◯ slide

I. ◯ table
    ◯ bridge
    ◯ bench

J. ◯ tires
    ◯ tree house
    ◯ tower

K. ◯ skateboard
    ◯ stroller
    ◯ bicycle

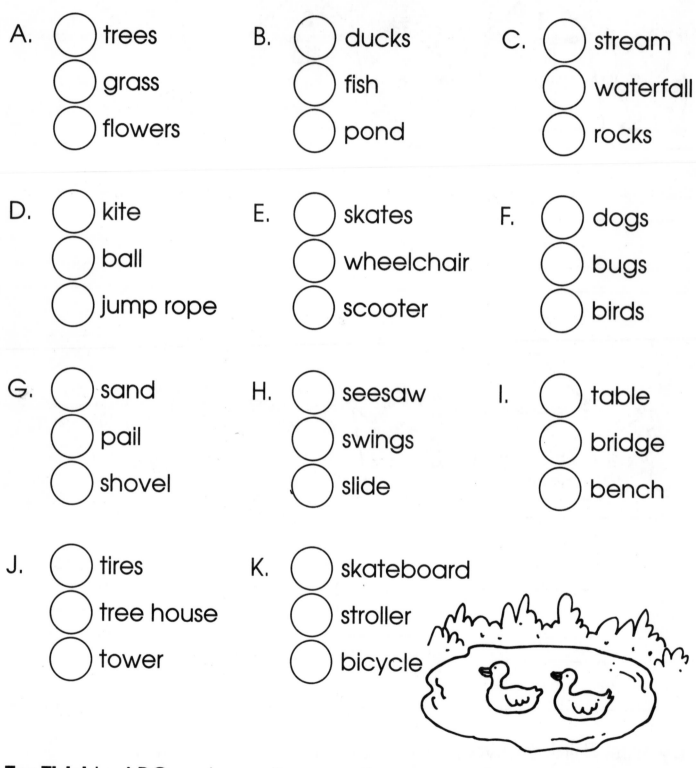

Try This! In ABC order, write your three favorite things to do.

One or Two?

Draw a line to match each word to its picture.

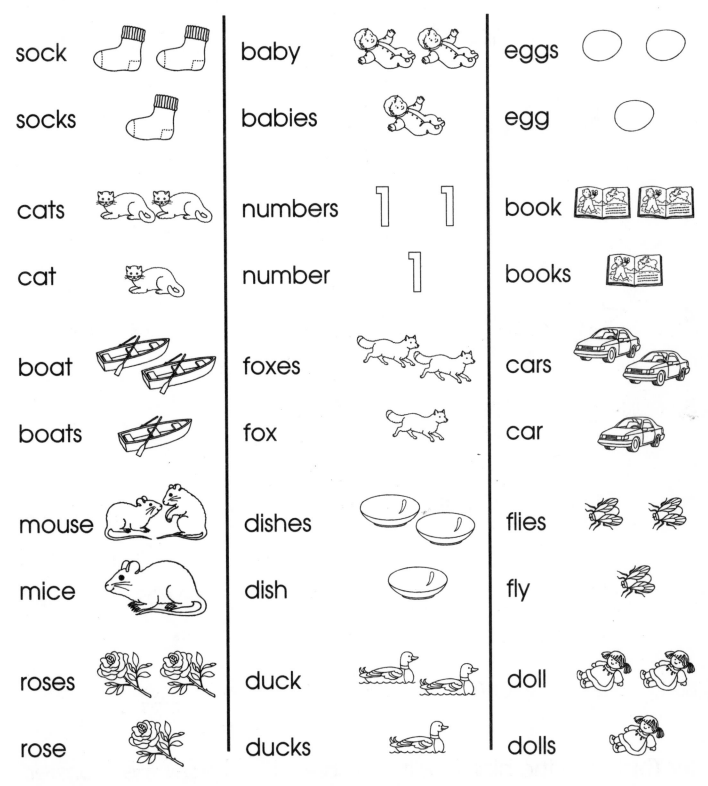

sock

socks

cats

cat

boat

boats

mouse

mice

roses

rose

baby

babies

numbers

number

foxes

fox

dishes

dish

duck

ducks

eggs

egg

book

books

cars

car

flies

fly

doll

dolls

Try This! Write **child** and **children**. Draw pictures to match.

FS-32056 First Grade Review

More Than One

Write the missing words that match the pictures.

1.   hand   h a n d s

2.   ball   _ _ _ _ _

3.   _ _ _ _   boxes

4.   star   _ _ _ _ _

5.   tree   _ _ _ _ _

6.   home   _ _ _ _ _

7.   _ _ _   eyes

8.   bird   _ _ _ _ _

Try This! Fill in the blanks with numbers. Then draw the monster.
The monster has ___ eyes, ___ mouths, ___ arms, and ___ legs.

48

Names, Names, Names

Write the names. Begin each with a capital letter.

james

mrs. yee

kyle

mr. larson

anna

sarah

nicole

joseph

ms. lopez

marco

miss ray

ian

Try This! Write your full name on the back of this paper.

You Pick the Name

Write a name in the blank. Begin each with a capital letter.

_____

1. _____ wants to be an astronaut.

2. _____ likes animals.

3. _____ is a very smart dog.

4. _____ and _____ are friends.

5. Mrs. _____ works at our school.

6. _____ is good at art.

7. I know someone named Mr. _____ .

8. My last name is _____ .

9. _____ likes to ride her bike.

10. _____ can sing really well.

Try This! Write your favorite name.

All Mixed-up!

Write the words in the correct order to make sentences. The first word in a sentence begins with a capital letter.

1.   are   big.   Whales _____

_____

2.   sea.   They   in   the   live

_____

3.   They   swim.   can

_____

4.   not   are   fish.   Whales

_____

5.   mammals.   They   are

_____

6.   drink   whales   milk.   Baby

_____

Try This! Write your own sentence about whales.

Kim's Kitten

Write the words in the correct
order to make sentences.
The first word in a sentence
begins with a capital letter.

1.   girl.   Kim   a   is

2.   very   is   She   smart.

3.   wanted   Kim   pet.   a

4.   She   kitten.   a   got

5.   kitten.   loved   her   Kim

6.   with   played   her   Kim   kitten.

Try This! What pet would you like? Write a sentence about it.

          FS-32056 First Grade Review

Name _____

A Trip to the Zoo

Read each sentence.
Circle the • if it is a telling sentence.
Circle the ? if it is an asking sentence.

1. We went to the zoo   (•)   ?

2. Have you been to a zoo   •   (?)

3. We saw lots of animals   •   ?

4. The elephants were big   •   ?

5. Next, we saw the giraffes   •   ?

6. Are you as tall as a giraffe •   ?

7. The monkeys were funny   •   ?

8. They chase each other   •   ?

9. Do you like to play chase   •   ?

10. What is your favorite animal •   ?

11. We liked the sea lions the best •   ?

12. They played in the water   •   ?

Try This! Write a telling sentence and an asking sentence about the zoo. Make sure to put a period (•) or a question mark (?) at the end.

53

Planting a Garden

Read each sentence.
Write a • at the end if it is a telling sentence.
Write a ? at the end if it is an asking sentence.

1. We are planting a garden.

2. Have you ever had a garden?

3. First, we need to pull up the weeds

4. Then we will make the soil loose

5. Have you ever seen a worm

6. There are lots of worms in the soil

7. Next, we will plant the seeds

8. What is your favorite vegetable

9. We are planting beans and carrots

10. We will also grow corn and peppers

11. Our garden needs sunshine and water

12. Would you like to plant a garden

Try This! Write an asking sentence about a garden. Give it to a partner to answer.

FS-32056 First Grade Review

Spelling Practice

Choose words you need to practice.
Write each word twice on the matching dogs.

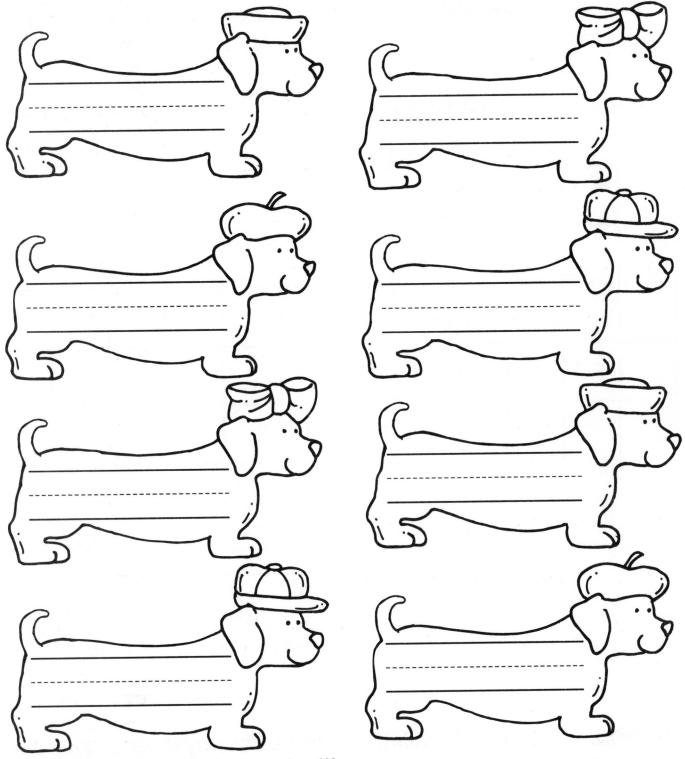

Try This! Trace each word with a crayon.

FS-32056 First Grade Review

Make a Spelling Puzzle

Choose spelling words you need to practice.
Write them in the empty puzzle.
Fill the extra boxes with letters.
Now look for your words and color them.
Write the words you found on the lines.

knot

Try This! Read each word. Then close your eyes and spell it aloud. Open your eyes and check. Did you spell it right?

Name _____

Plan a Story

1. What kind of story do you want to write?
   Fill in all the circles that answer the question:
   ○ true
   ○ make-believe that could really happen
   ○ make-believe that couldn't really happen
   ○ funny
   ○ serious
   ○ scary
   ○ other _____

2. What kind of characters will you have?
   Fill in all the circles that answer the question:
   ○ people I know
   ○ people I make up
   ○ animals I know
   ○ animals I make up
   ○ make-believe creatures

   Write the names of your characters.

   _____
   -
   _____
   -
   _____

Try This! Where will your story take place? Draw it on the back.

Story Ideas

What do you want to happen in your story?
Write three ideas.
Draw a star by your favorite one.

1. _____

2. _____

3. _____

What would be
a good title for
your story?

_____

Try This! Meet with a partner. Read and listen to each other's
ideas. Ask your partner which idea he or she likes best.

My Trip

Think of a trip that you went on. Draw a picture of your favorite part of the trip. Then write a sentence describing it.

_____

- -

_____

- -

_____

- -

_____

Try This! Write where you would like to go on a trip.

FS-32056 First Grade Review

Think Back

What is your favorite thing to do at school?
Draw a picture of it. Then write about it.

Try This! Read what you wrote. Did you leave out any words?

Friendly Questions

Meet with a partner.
Think of questions to ask each other.
Write the questions. Then trade papers. Write your answers.

Question

_____
_____
_____
_____

Answer

_____
_____
_____
_____

Question

_____
_____
_____
_____

Answer

_____
_____
_____
_____

Try This! Which do you like better—asking or answering? Why?

Nice to Meet You

Yikes! A talking dinosaur just
entered your classroom.
Write two questions you will ask it.
Then write its answers.

Question

_____

_____

_____

Answer

_____

_____

Question

_____

_____

_____

Answer

_____

_____

Try This! Write a question the dinosaur might ask you.

FS-32056 First Grade Review

A Tasty Tea Party

The Big Bad Wolf is having a tea party.
He's hoping to eat any little pigs that show up!
The party will be held in the deep, dark forest.
It will be on Friday, May 5, at 10 o'clock.

Write the invitation.

Please come
to my tea
party!

Date _____

_____

Time _____

_____

Place _____

_____

Given by _____

Try This! Pretend you are a pig. Send your reply to the wolf.

Come to My Party!

Pretend you are having a party at your house.
It can be any kind of party you want.
Write the invitation.
Draw pictures to decorate it.

What _____

Date _____

Time _____

Place _____

Given by _____

Try This! Make a list of the things you would need to do to get ready for your party.

Folk Tale Thank-you Note

Choose a folk tale you know. Think of how one character helped another. Example:

The woodcutter saved Little Red Riding Hood.

Pretend you are the character who was helped. Write a thank-you note to the other character.

Thank you!

Try This! Whom could you make a thank-you note for? Write the person's name and what you would thank him or her for.

FS-32056 First Grade Review

Thank You!

Think of someone who has helped you lately.
Write him or her a thank-you note.

Thank you!

Try This! Cut out your note. Glue it to a piece of colored paper. Trim the edges. Give it to your helper.

Check Your Writing

Write a story. Work with a partner.
Color the pencil after you do each step.

1 Read aloud what you wrote.
Listen for these things:
- missing words
- extra words
- parts that don't make sense

2 Read aloud what you wrote.
Look for these things:
- a capital letter at the beginning of each sentence
- a punctuation mark (. or **?** or **!**) at the end of each sentence

3 Read aloud what you wrote.
Look for this:
- words that are spelled wrong

  knight

Partner's name _____

Try This! Would you rather work alone or with a partner? Why?

X Marks the Spot

Write a story. Do this page when you finish writing.
Mark an **X** in the **Yes** or **No** column as you answer
each question.
Fix the parts that need it.

Yes	No	
		Are there any missing words or extra words?
		Do all sentences make sense?
		Do you want to add anything else?
		Do all names and sentences begin with a capital letter?
		Do all sentences end with a punctuation mark (. or **!** or **?**)?
		Are there any words you need help spelling?

Try This! Are any words too sloppy to read? If yes, fix them.

That Doesn't Belong!

Cross out the word that doesn't belong.
Write a new word for each group.

1. **Pets**
bird
rabbit
snow
fish
_____
- - - - - - - - - - -
_____

2. **School**
book
cloud
pencil
teacher
_____
- - - - - - - - - - -
_____

3. **Numbers**
cheese
seven
one
three
_____
- - - - - - - - - - -
_____

4. **Colors**
box
black
yellow
purple
_____
- - - - - - - - - - -
_____

5. **Family**
dad
baby
tape
sister
_____
- - - - - - - - - - -
_____

6. **Home**
bed
couch
lamp
shark
_____
- - - - - - - - - - -
_____

7. **Outside**
flower
butterfly
river
desk
_____
- - - - - - - - - - -
_____

8. **Food**
pizza
six
salad
bread
_____
- - - - - - - - - - -
_____

9. **Space**
rocket
moon
bike
star
_____
- - - - - - - - - - -
_____

Try This! List four things that would fit in a **Toys** group.

Name the Group

Write a title that names each group of pictures.

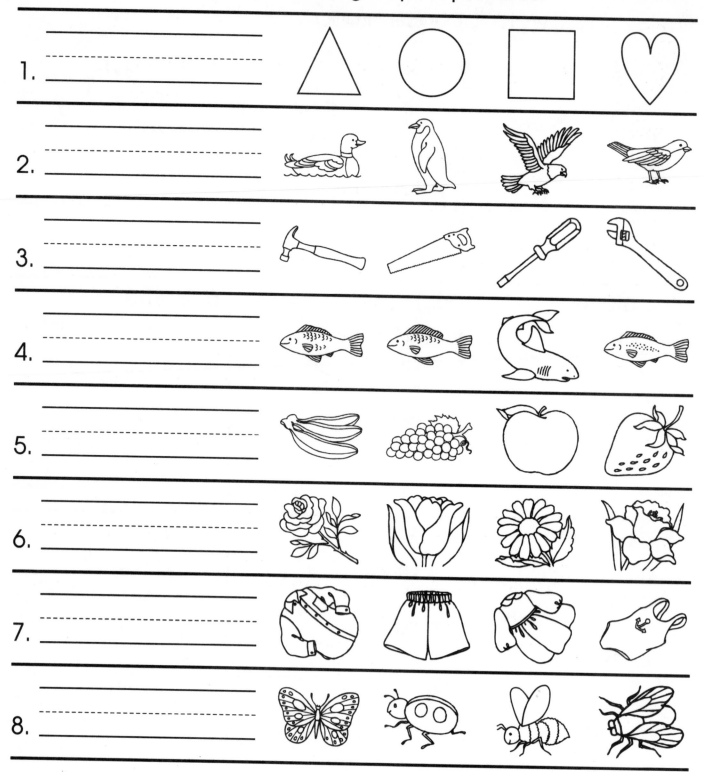

1. _____

2. _____

3. _____

4. _____

5. _____

6. _____

7. _____

8. _____

Try This! Draw another picture for each row.

70

Alike and Different

How are a globe and a ball alike?

_____

- - - - - - - - - - - - - - - - - - - -

_____

How are they different?

_____

- - - - - - - - - - - - - - - - - - - -

_____

How are you and a pencil alike?

_____

- - - - - - - - - - - - - - - - - - - -

_____

How are you different?

_____

- - - - - - - - - - - - - - - - - - - -

_____

Try This! Name something else that is like you and the pencil.

FS-32056 First Grade Review

At the Farm

Use words from the picture for the first two blanks.
Then finish each sentence.

tree

barn

house

duck

chick   hen

sheep

cow

pig

horse

pond

1. A _____ is like a _____ because
_____
_____

2. A _____ is like a _____ because
_____
_____

3. A _____ is like a _____ because
_____
_____

Try This! Who in your family is most like you? Why?

Watch Us Grow

Draw the missing pictures.
Number the boxes **1**, **2**, and **3** to show the order.

Try This! Work with a friend. Draw how a butterfly grows.

FS-32056 First Grade Review

First, Next, Then, Last

Number the boxes **1**, **2**, **3**, and **4** to show the order.

Try This! How do you go to bed? Draw and number the steps.

74

FS-32056 First Grade Review

Busy Bear's Bad Day

Draw a line to match each set of boxes.

Cause   **Effect**

Busy Bear sleeps late.	He screams.
Busy Bear forgets his lunch.	He misses the bus.
Busy Bear pounds his thumb.	He is hungry.
Busy Bear rides too fast.	His family cheers him up.
Busy Bear feels bad.	He hits a tree.

Try This! Finish this sentence: **Once I had to ___ because I ___.**

What Might Happen?

Draw a picture that shows what might happen.

What might happen if your umbrella had a hole?	
What might happen if your teacher got the chicken pox?	
What might happen if you ate too much candy?	

Try This! Draw a silly picture (example: an upside-down farm). Write three things that could have caused it.

How's the Weather?

Fill in the circle of the sentence that matches the picture.

1. ○ It just rained.
   ○ It just snowed.

2. ○ It is warm.
   ○ It is cold.

3. ○ There is a light breeze.
   ○ There is a strong wind.

4. ○ It is quiet outside.
   ○ It is noisy outside.

5. ○ It is sunny.
   ○ It is cloudy.

6. ○ It is safe to go out.
   ○ It is not safe to go out.

Try This! Do you think it is warm or cold outside? Why?

How Do They Feel?

Fill in the circles of the sentences that could match the picture.

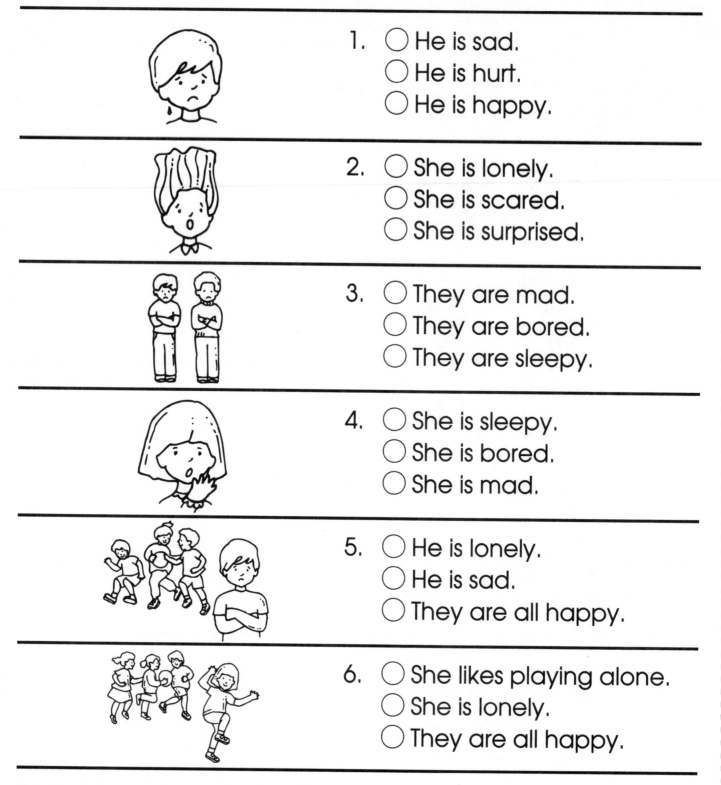

1. ○ He is sad.
   ○ He is hurt.
   ○ He is happy.

2. ○ She is lonely.
   ○ She is scared.
   ○ She is surprised.

3. ○ They are mad.
   ○ They are bored.
   ○ They are sleepy.

4. ○ She is sleepy.
   ○ She is bored.
   ○ She is mad.

5. ○ He is lonely.
   ○ He is sad.
   ○ They are all happy.

6. ○ She likes playing alone.
   ○ She is lonely.
   ○ They are all happy.

Try This! What are two ways you are feeling now?

Sea Life

Use words from the picture for the first two blanks.
Then finish each sentence.

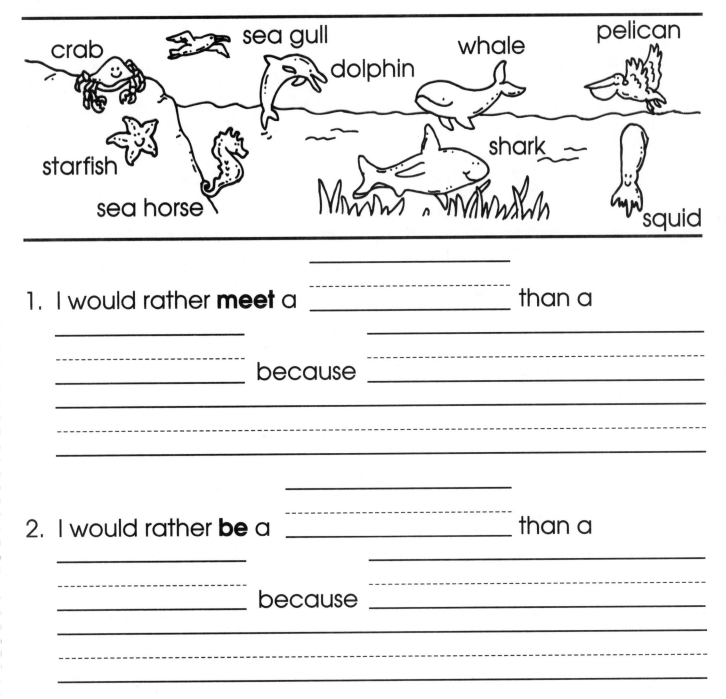

1. I would rather **meet** a _____ than a

   _____ because _____

   _____

2. I would rather **be** a _____ than a

   _____ because _____

   _____

Try This! What is your favorite sea animal? Why?

79

A Long Time Ago

Use words from the picture for the first two blanks.
Then finish each sentence.

castle

forest

princess

horse

knight

dragon

cave

1. I would rather **meet** a _____ than a

_____ because _____

_____

2. I would rather **be** a _____ than a

_____ because _____

_____

Try This! Would you rather live now or in the time of castles?
Write why.

Name _____

What's Missing?

Write the missing numbers.

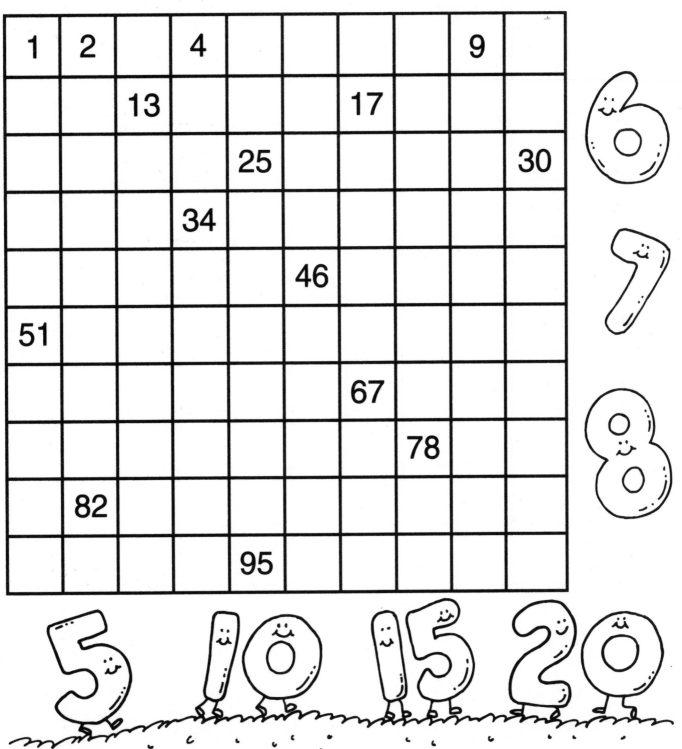

1	2		4					9	
		13				17			
				25					30
			34						
					46				
51									
						67			
							78		
	82								
				95					

Try This! Point to the numbers on the chart as you count by fives to 100.

81

FS-32056 First Grade Review

Name_____

Number Chart

Fill in the number chart from 1 to 100.

1									

Try This! Move your index finger down the last column to count by tens to 100.

FS-32056 First Grade Review

Liftoff!

Count by tens.
Connect the dots from 10 to 100.
Begin at the ★.

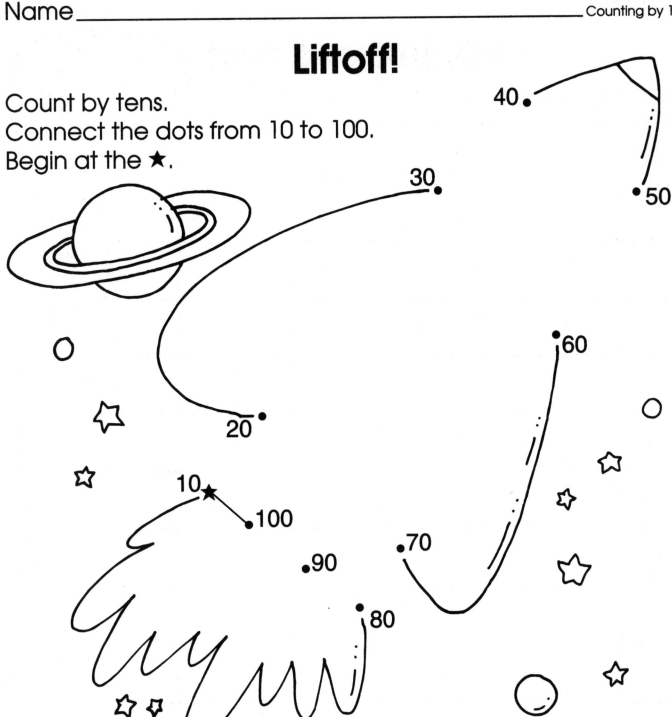

Count by tens. Write the missing numbers.

10, 20, _____, _____, 50, _____, _____, _____, 90, _____

Try This! Count backwards by tens from 100 to 10.

FS-32056 First Grade Review

Up, Up, and Away

Count by fives. Connect the dots from 5 to 100.
Begin at the star ★.

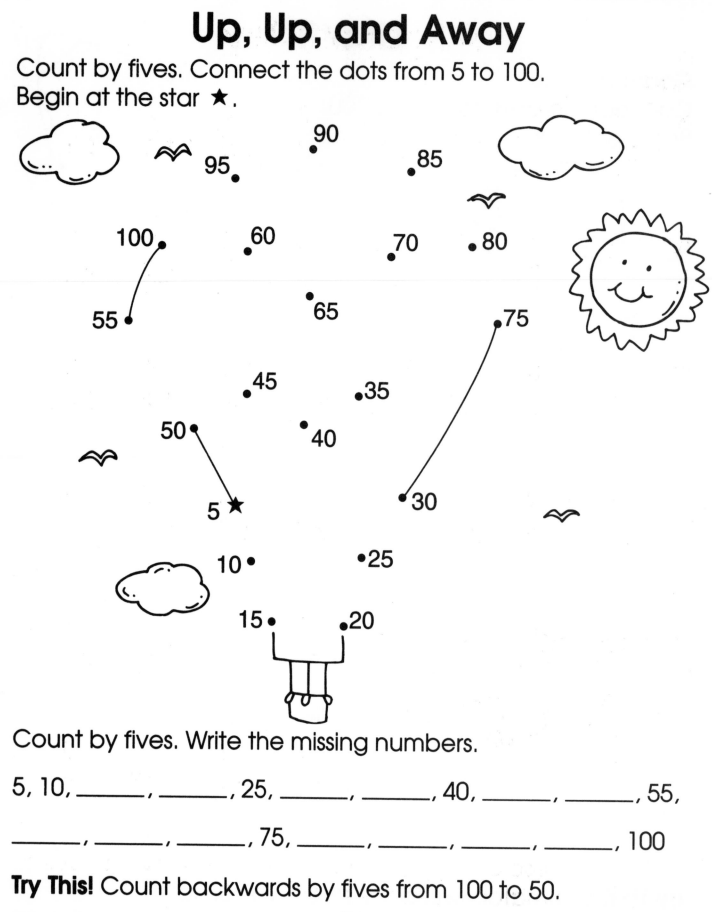

Count by fives. Write the missing numbers.

5, 10, _____, _____, 25, _____, _____, 40, _____, _____, 55,

_____, _____, _____, 75, _____, _____, _____, _____, 100

Try This! Count backwards by fives from 100 to 50.

FS-32056 First Grade Review

Alligator Alley

Add.

A.

5	3	6	8	2	9	7	0
+2	+1	+4	+9	+6	+0	+7	+5

B.

1	4	5	3	6	8	9	9
+1	+8	+9	+6	+0	+7	+9	+3

C.

7	0	1	4	5	3	6	8
+3	+2	+9	+4	+1	+0	+6	+2

D.

5	9	0	1	2	4	7	9
+8	+4	+4	+6	+3	+7	+5	+6

E.

2	9	3	1
+2	+2	+8	+7

F.

4	6	7	8
+3	+8	+9	+8

Try This! Choose a problem and circle it. Draw two groups of alligators to match the problem.

85

Play Ball!

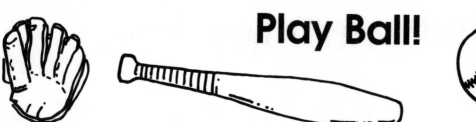

Add.

A. 4 + 2 = _____	7 + 6 = _____	8 + 1 = _____
B. 0 + 7 = _____	3 + 5 = _____	9 + 9 = _____
C. 1 + 2 = _____	6 + 3 = _____	7 + 4 = _____
D. 2 + 7 = _____	4 + 1 = _____	0 + 1 = _____
E. 5 + 5 = _____	8 + 6 = _____	6 + 9 = _____
F. 9 + 1 = _____	5 + 7 = _____	4 + 6 = _____
G. 7 + 8 = _____	9 + 5 = _____	1 + 3 = _____
H. 6 + 5 = _____	0 + 8 = _____	2 + 9 = _____
I. 8 + 4 = _____	5 + 0 = _____	5 + 4 = _____
J. 3 + 3 = _____	9 + 8 = _____	3 + 7 = _____
K. 4 + 9 = _____	1 + 5 = _____	3 + 2 = _____
L. 3 + 4 = _____	9 + 7 = _____	8 + 3 = _____
M. 2 + 8 = _____	6 + 2 = _____	3 + 9 = _____

Try This! Write four problems whose answers are 10.

                     FS-32056 First Grade Review

Name _____

Rainy Day

Add.

A.
15	30	64	58	20	19	32	40
+ 32	+ 61	+ 24	+ 10	+ 16	+ 40	+ 47	+ 53
47							

B.
71	60	53	12	70	85	37	19
+ 21	+ 39	+ 43	+ 76	+ 10	+ 13	+ 50	+ 60

C.
43	54	12	4	15	21	62	70
+ 31	+ 2	+ 85	+ 40	+ 20	+ 70	+ 14	+ 22

D.
53	36	20	41	22	43	30	14
+ 32	+ 60	+ 24	+ 58	+ 53	+ 40	+ 25	+ 61

E.
41	32	67	50
+ 45	+ 62	+ 22	+ 27

F.
54	40	72	36
+ 43	+ 18	+ 20	+ 62

Try This! Do these in your head: **60 + 30 = ___**   **22 + 55 = ___**

FS-32056 First Grade Review

Elephant Parade

Add.

A.
$$23 + 63$$ $$39 + 60$$ $$14 + 64$$ $$57 + 10$$ $$23 + 15$$ $$40 + 50$$ $$32 + 44$$ $$85 + 10$$

B.
$$62 + 35$$ $$61 + 8$$ $$55 + 32$$ $$11 + 73$$ $$12 + 42$$ $$3 + 80$$ $$46 + 12$$ $$25 + 34$$

C.
$$18 + 80$$ $$84 + 12$$ $$30 + 67$$ $$52 + 40$$ $$23 + 11$$ $$47 + 31$$ $$71 + 20$$ $$80 + 12$$

D.
$$50 + 31$$ $$32 + 57$$ $$10 + 55$$ $$73 + 22$$ $$46 + 51$$ $$54 + 40$$ $$10 + 69$$ $$11 + 65$$

E.
$$34 + 53$$ $$61 + 11$$ $$60 + 23$$ $$41 + 42$$ $$87 + 12$$ $$30 + 54$$ $$15 + 74$$ $$60 + 36$$

Try This! Make up a problem whose answer is **20 elephants**.

FS-32056 First Grade Review

At the Beach

Subtract.

A.	6 -2	9 -3	3 -2	9 -7	10 -5	10 -1	15 -8	11 -5
B.	12 -4	6 -3	13 -9	7 -4	12 -7	13 -6	8 -5	7 -7
C.	5 -1	14 -6	10 -8	14 -5	8 -8	5 -0	17 -8	6 -5
D.	4 -3	11 -9	11 -4	1 -1	5 -2	11 -3	12 -9	16 -7

E.	8 -2	9 -1	18 -9	9 -4

F.	10 -7	16 -8	10 -6	14 -7

Try This! Circle all problems whose answer is your age.

FS-32056 First Grade Review

Name _____

Shining Stars

Subtract.

A. 7 – 3 = _____   14 – 8 = _____   16 – 9 = _____

B. 8 – 7 = _____   11 – 8 = _____   11 – 2 = _____

C. 4 – 2 = _____   15 – 6 = _____   12 – 5 = _____

D. 7 – 6 = _____   13 – 4 = _____   11 – 7 = _____

E. 5 – 3 = _____   17 – 8 = _____   10 – 2 = _____

F. 4 – 4 = _____   13 – 8 = _____   12 – 6 = _____

G. 3 – 0 = _____   10 – 9 = _____   10 – 3 = _____

H. 6 – 1 = _____   12 – 3 = _____   17 – 9 = _____

I. 8 – 4 = _____   18 – 9 = _____   10 – 4 = _____

J. 2 – 2 = _____   15 – 7 = _____   16 – 8 = _____

K. 9 – 6 = _____   14 – 9 = _____   10 – 5 = _____

L. 2 – 1 = _____   12 – 8 = _____   11 – 6 = _____

M. 7 – 2 = _____   14 – 7 = _____   13 – 7 = _____

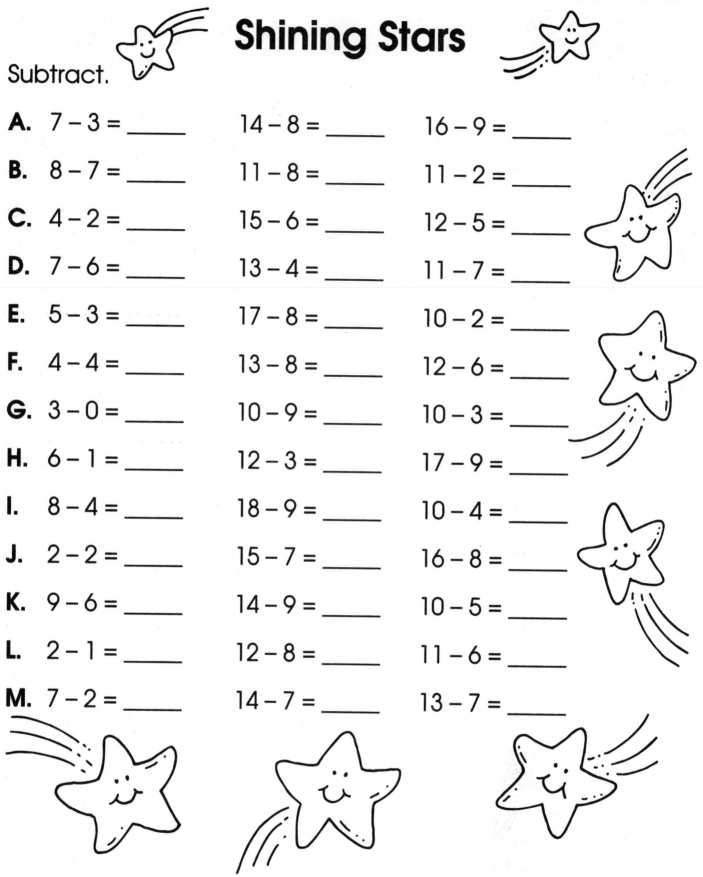

Try This! Write two subtraction problems using **5**, **7**, and **12**.

FS-32056 First Grade Review

Name _____

Spring Flowers

Subtract.

A.
$$83 - 63 = 20$$
$$69 - 30$$
$$76 - 64$$
$$57 - 10$$
$$96 - 15$$
$$40 - 30$$
$$25 - 14$$

B.
$$39 - 13$$
$$36 - 6$$
$$41 - 40$$
$$57 - 21$$
$$62 - 10$$
$$85 - 50$$
$$39 - 24$$

C.
$$81 - 71$$
$$84 - 40$$
$$78 - 52$$
$$99 - 28$$
$$25 - 23$$
$$47 - 17$$
$$83 - 30$$

D.
$$96 - 90$$
$$87 - 14$$
$$29 - 7$$
$$74 - 32$$
$$98 - 60$$
$$56 - 52$$
$$79 - 25$$

E.
$$89 - 82$$
$$65 - 34$$
$$98 - 43$$
$$73 - 22$$
$$45 - 10$$
$$91 - 31$$
$$80 - 60$$

Try This! Check your work by adding your answer to the number subtracted. (Example: 83 − 63 = 20; 20 + 63 = 83)

FS-32056 First Grade Review

Name _____

Gone Fishing!

Subtract.

A.

91	82	39	48	76	95	47
− 60	− 52	− 28	− 23	− 16	− 30	− 14

B.

49	86	71	59	92	85	39
− 32	− 21	− 51	− 41	− 90	− 72	− 14

C.

67	78	36	90	82	54	76
− 40	− 28	− 32	− 70	− 41	− 10	− 63

D.

68	73	88	49
− 51	− 30	− 4	− 46

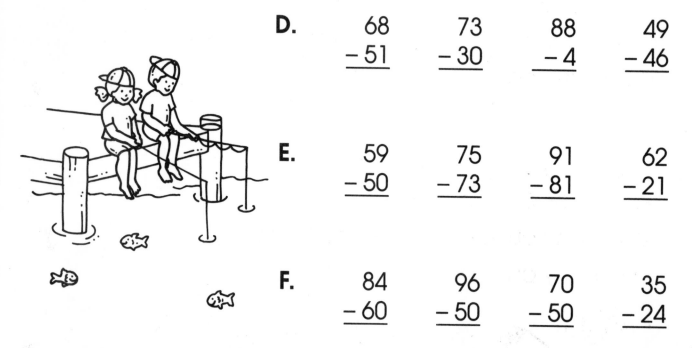

E.

59	75	91	62
− 50	− 73	− 81	− 21

F.

84	96	70	35
− 60	− 50	− 50	− 24

Try This! Write a subtraction problem whose answer is **13 fish.**

92

Guess and Check

A. Maria and Ann have 7 books in all.
Ann has 3 more than Maria.

How many books does Ann have?   _____

How many books does Maria have?   _____

B. Lynn and Sam have 9 dinosaurs in all.
Lynn has 1 more than Sam.

How many dinosaurs does Lynn have? _____

How many dinosaurs does Sam have?   _____

C. Matt and Hannah have 10 cars in all.
Hannah has 2 more than Matt.

How many cars does Matt have?   _____

How many cars does Hannah have?   _____

D. Jessica and Danny have 12 cubes in all.
Danny has 4 more than Jessica.

How many cubes does Jessica have? _____

How many cubes does Danny have?   _____

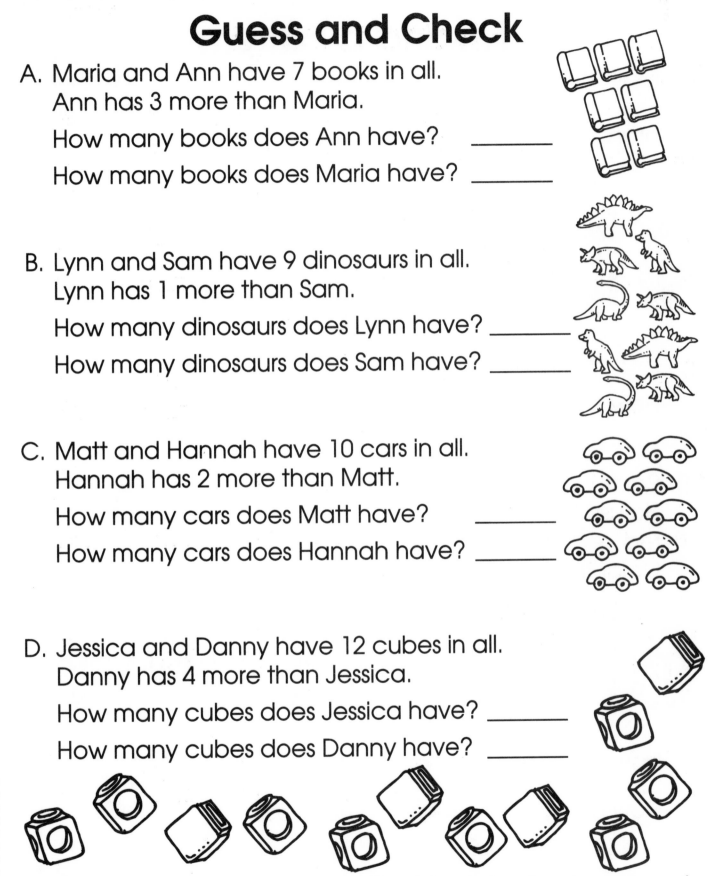

Try This! Act out the problems with objects to check your work.

Finding a Pattern

A. Mary planted a row of 9 daisies.
She used this color pattern:
orange, purple, purple, orange, purple, purple.
Color the daisies to match the pattern.

How many orange daisies did she plant?_____

How many purple daisies did she plant?_____

B. Paul planted a row of 12 tulips.
He used this color pattern:
red, red, yellow, red, red, yellow.
Color the tulips to match the pattern.

How many red tulips did he plant?_____

How many yellow tulips did he plant?_____

Try This! Draw and color a row of flowers to make a new pattern.

94

Name_____

Number Patterns

Find the number pattern.
Write the missing numbers.

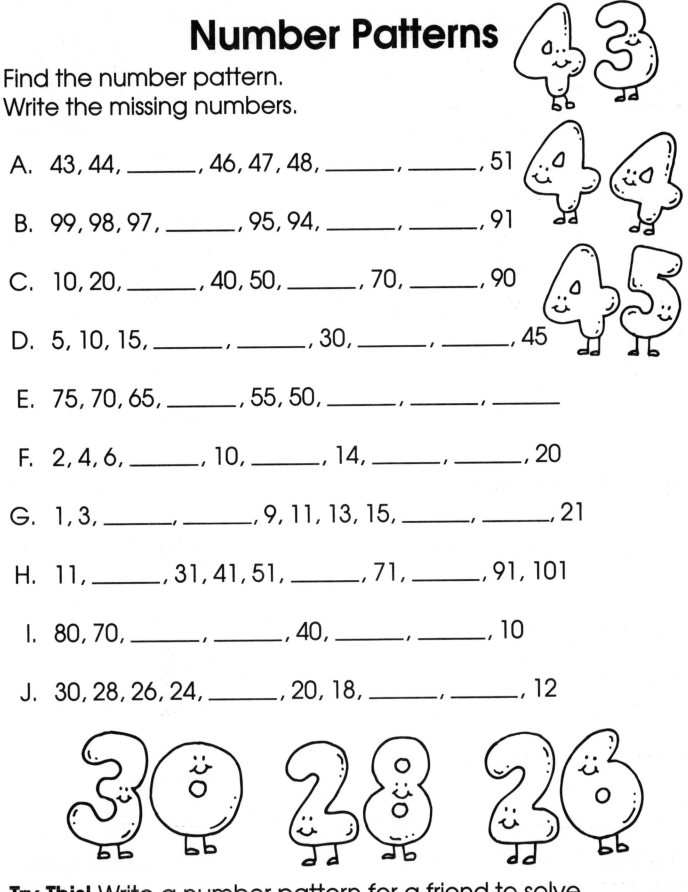

A. 43, 44, _____, 46, 47, 48, _____, _____, 51

B. 99, 98, 97, _____, 95, 94, _____, _____, 91

C. 10, 20, _____, 40, 50, _____, 70, _____, 90

D. 5, 10, 15, _____, _____, 30, _____, _____, 45

E. 75, 70, 65, _____, 55, 50, _____, _____, _____

F. 2, 4, 6, _____, 10, _____, 14, _____, _____, 20

G. 1, 3, _____, _____, 9, 11, 13, 15, _____, _____, 21

H. 11, _____, 31, 41, 51, _____, 71, _____, 91, 101

I. 80, 70, _____, _____, 40, _____, _____, 10

J. 30, 28, 26, 24, _____, 20, 18, _____, _____, 12

Try This! Write a number pattern for a friend to solve.

FS-32056 First Grade Review

What Comes Next?

Find the number pattern.
Write the missing numbers.

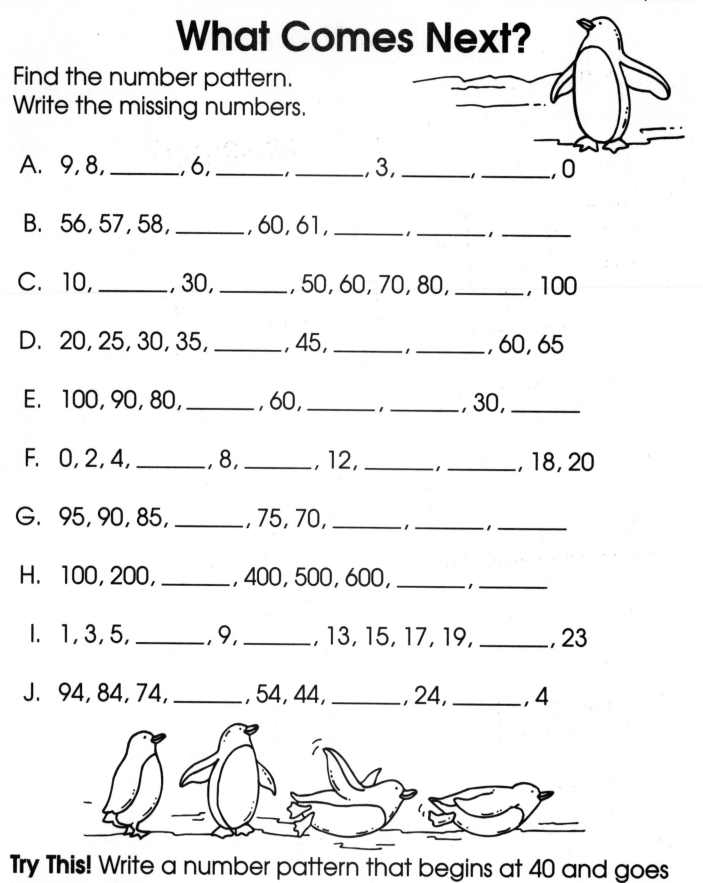

A. 9, 8, _____, 6, _____, _____, 3, _____, _____, 0

B. 56, 57, 58, _____, 60, 61, _____, _____, _____

C. 10, _____, 30, _____, 50, 60, 70, 80, _____, 100

D. 20, 25, 30, 35, _____, 45, _____, _____, 60, 65

E. 100, 90, 80, _____, 60, _____, _____, 30, _____

F. 0, 2, 4, _____, 8, _____, 12, _____, _____, 18, 20

G. 95, 90, 85, _____, 75, 70, _____, _____, _____

H. 100, 200, _____, 400, 500, 600, _____, _____

I. 1, 3, 5, _____, 9, _____, 13, 15, 17, 19, _____, 23

J. 94, 84, 74, _____, 54, 44, _____, 24, _____, 4

Try This! Write a number pattern that begins at 40 and goes backwards.

Equal Parts

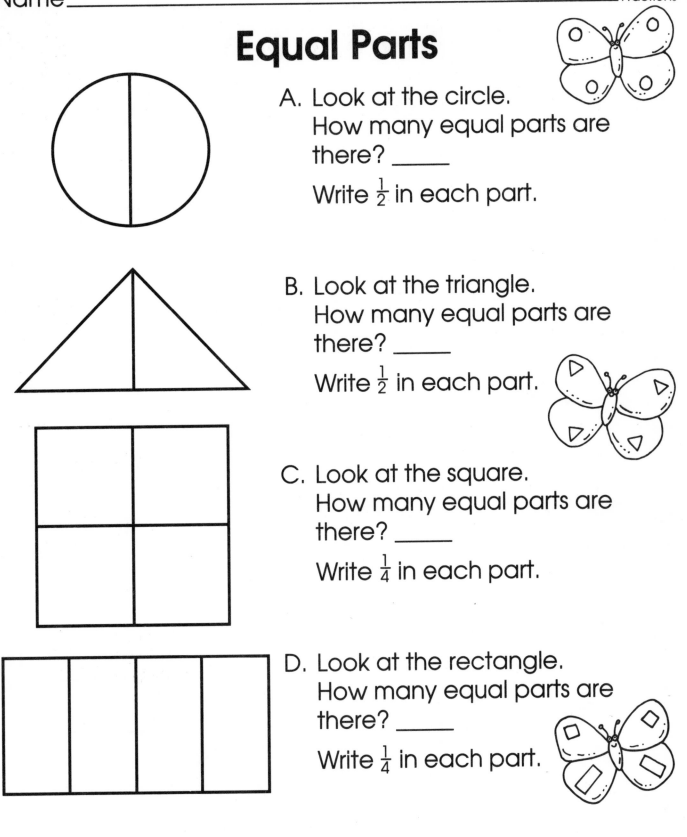

A. Look at the circle.
How many equal parts are
there? _____

Write $\frac{1}{2}$ in each part.

B. Look at the triangle.
How many equal parts are
there? _____

Write $\frac{1}{2}$ in each part.

C. Look at the square.
How many equal parts are
there? _____

Write $\frac{1}{4}$ in each part.

D. Look at the rectangle.
How many equal parts are
there? _____

Write $\frac{1}{4}$ in each part.

Try This! Draw three squares. Find different ways to divide
them into fourths (four equal parts).

Fraction Fun

A. Color $\frac{1}{2}$ red.
   Color $\frac{1}{2}$ blue.

B. Color $\frac{1}{2}$ yellow.
   Color $\frac{1}{2}$ green.

C. Color $\frac{1}{2}$ blue.
   Color $\frac{1}{2}$ green.

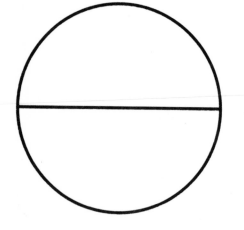 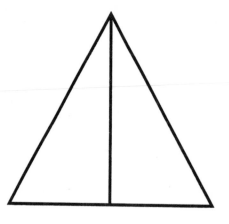 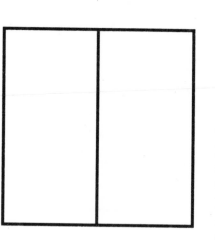

D. Color $\frac{1}{4}$ red.
   Color $\frac{3}{4}$ yellow.

E. Color $\frac{3}{4}$ blue.
   Color $\frac{1}{4}$ yellow.

F. Color $\frac{1}{4}$ blue.
   Color $\frac{2}{4}$ green.
   Color $\frac{1}{4}$ red.

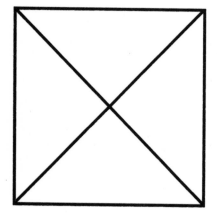 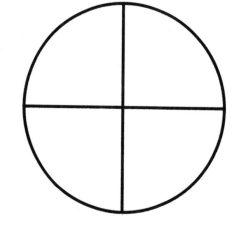 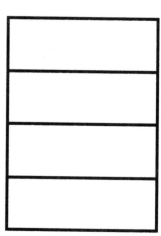

Try This! Draw a heart. Color $\frac{1}{2}$ purple. Color $\frac{1}{2}$ red.

FS-32056 First Grade Review

Wiggly Worms

Measure each worm with your fingertip.
Write how many fingertips long it is.

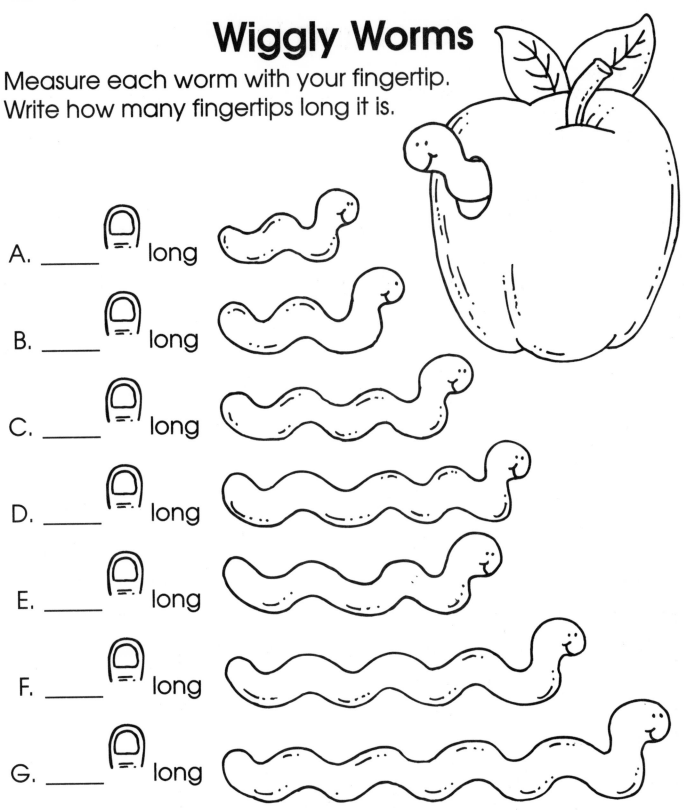

A. _____ long

B. _____ long

C. _____ long

D. _____ long

E. _____ long

F. _____ long

G. _____ long

Try This! Measure something in your room with your fingertip.

99

FS-32056 First Grade Review

How Long Is It?

Fill in the circle next to the correct answer.

A. How many centimeters long is the crayon?
- ○ 6 cm
- ○ 8 cm
- ○ 10 cm

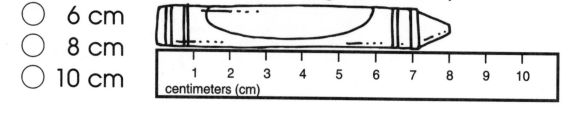

B. How many centimeters long is the pencil?
- ○ 6 cm
- ○ 8 cm
- ○ 10 cm

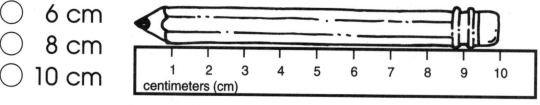

C. How many centimeters long is the sharpener?
- ○ 1 cm
- ○ 2 cm
- ○ 3 cm

D. How many centimeters long is the eraser?
- ○ 1 cm
- ○ 2 cm
- ○ 3 cm

E. How many centimeters long is the paper clip?
- ○ 4 cm
- ○ 6 cm
- ○ 7 cm

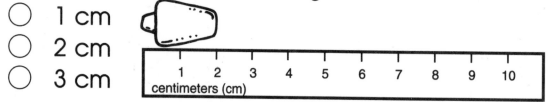

Try This! Write the five objects in order from shortest to longest.

FS-32056 First Grade Review

Name_____

What Time Is It?

Write the time.

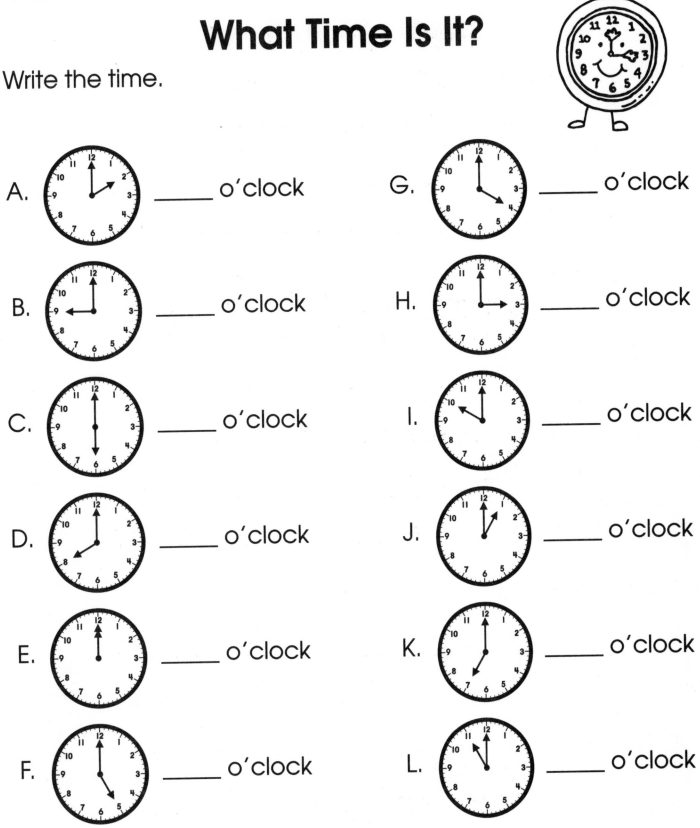

A. _____ o'clock

B. _____ o'clock

C. _____ o'clock

D. _____ o'clock

E. _____ o'clock

F. _____ o'clock

G. _____ o'clock

H. _____ o'clock

I. _____ o'clock

J. _____ o'clock

K. _____ o'clock

L. _____ o'clock

Try This! When do you go to bed? Write the time.

101

Name_____

Clock Match-up

Draw a line from each clock to
the clock with the matching time.

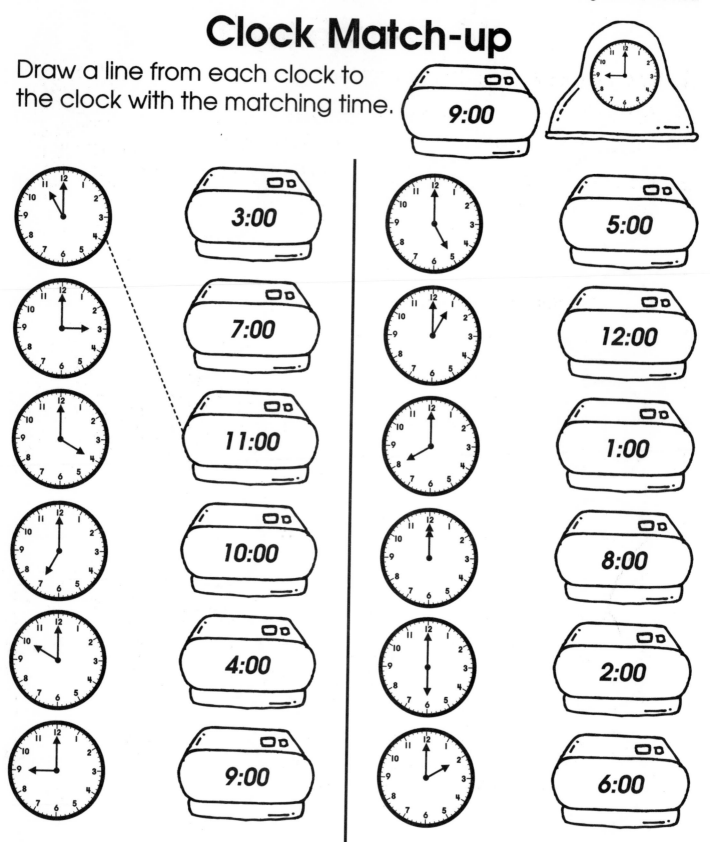

Try This! Look at the clock in your room. Color the clock
above whose time is closest to the time your clock shows.

Make a Graph

1. Ask 8 classmates this question:

   Which of these do you like to play on the most—the swings, the slide, or the bars?

2. Start with the bottom box in each column and color a box for each answer.

Favorite Play Graph

Swings   Slide   Bars

Try This! Read your graph. What do your classmates like to play on most?

FS-32056 First Grade Review

Name_____

Zoo Animal Graph

Some children voted for their favorite animal.
Read the graph. Answer the questions.

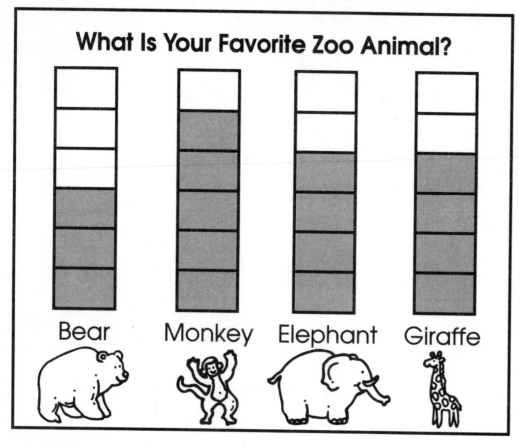

What Is Your Favorite Zoo Animal?

Bear Monkey Elephant Giraffe

1. Which animal did the
   children like the most? _____

2. Which animal did the
   children like the least? _____

3. Which animal got
   the same number of
   votes as the giraffe? _____

Try This! Color in a box to add your vote to the graph.

104   FS-32056 First Grade Review

Answer Key

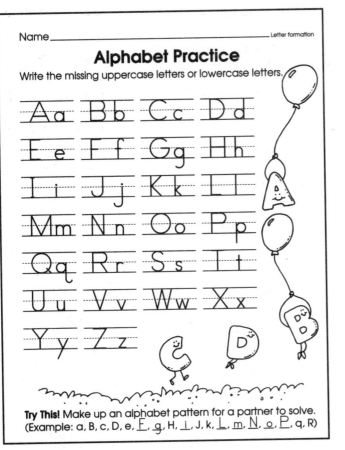

Alphabet Practice

Write the missing uppercase letters or lowercase letters.

Try This! Make up an alphabet pattern for a partner to solve.
(Example: a, B, c, D, e, _F_, _g_, H, _i_, J, k, _L_, _m_, _N_, _o_, _P_, q, R)

Page 1

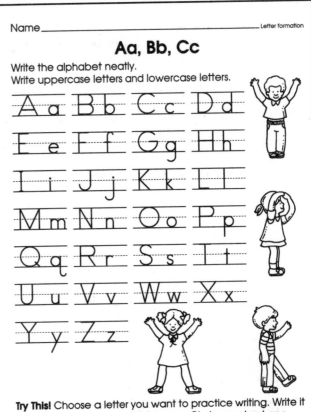

Aa, Bb, Cc

Write the alphabet neatly.
Write uppercase letters and lowercase letters.

Try This! Choose a letter you want to practice writing. Write it five times on the back of this paper. Circle your best one.

Page 2

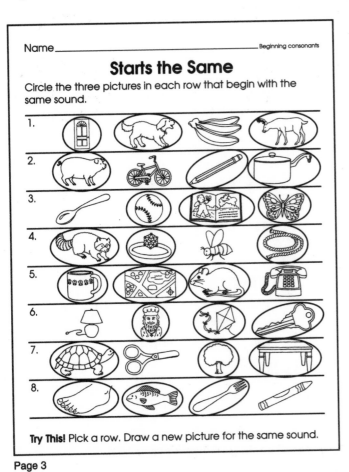

Starts the Same

Circle the three pictures in each row that begin with the same sound.

Try This! Pick a row. Draw a new picture for the same sound.

Page 3

What Sound Does It Begin With?

Look at the picture. What sound does it begin with?
Fill in the circle next to the matching letter.

Try This! Pick a letter. Name a word that starts with that sound.

Page 4

Answer Key

Consonant L blends

Name_____

Fun With Blends

Write the missing blend: **bl, cl, fl, gl, pl,** or **sl.**

1.  **cl** ock
2. **gl** obe
3. **fl** ag
4. **pl** ant
5. **bl** ock
6. **gl** ue
7. **sl** ide
8. **fl** ute

9. **fl** ower
10. **cl** oud
11. **pl** anet
12. **sl** ed
13. **bl** anket
14. **cl** own
15. **gl** ove
16. **pl** ane

Try This! Use **L** blends to write five words that end with **ow**.

Page 5

Consonant R blends

Name_____

Which Blend?

Write the missing blend: **br, dr, gr, pr,** or **tr.**

1. Things that go
tr ain
tr uck
tr actor

3. Colors
gr een
br own
gr ay

5. Instruments
tr umpet
dr um
tr iangle

2. Food
gr apes
br ead
pr etzel

4. Things outside
tr ee
br idge
gr ound

6. People
gr andma
br other
pr ince

Try This! How many words can you write that rhyme with **train**?

Page 6

Digraphs—ch, sh, th

Name_____

Puzzle Fun

Fill in the blank with **ch, sh,** or **th.**
Find and circle each word in the puzzle.

1. **ch** air
2. **sh** ell
3. **th** ree
4. **ch** est
5. **sh** eep
6. **sh** oe
7. **ch** ain
8. **th** umb

```
s k u c (s h o e) t
h (c (t h u m b) p h
e h o (c h e s t) r
l a (s h e e p) y e
l i m p d o n e e
f n u g (c h a i r)
```

Try This! Write five more words that start with **ch, sh,** or **th.**

Page 7

Silent consonants

Name_____

Silent Consonants

These words all have silent consonants.
Color the boxes of the consonants you do not hear.

1. w r i t e
2. c l i m b
3. l i g h t
4. w a l k
5. i s l a n d
6. k n e e
7. s i g n
8. s n o w
9. s c i e n c e
10. g h o s t

Try This! Write three words that begin with **kn**.

Page 8

FS-32056 First Grade Review

Answer Key

Short vowels

Which Vowel?

Write the missing short vowel: **a, e, i, o,** or **u.**

1. p i g
2. c u p
3. n e st
4. p o t
5. b u g
6. d u ck
7. p i n
8. sh e ll

9. h a t
10. ch i ck
11. f a n
12. r u g
13. m o p
14. fr o g
15. b e d
16. l o ck

Try This! Change the vowel in **b __ g** to make five different words.

Page 9

Name_____ Short vowels

Step by Step

1. Short **a** words: Draw a ○ around the pictures.
2. Short **e** words: Draw an **X** on the pictures.
3. Short **i** words: Draw a □ around the pictures.
4. Short **o** words: Draw a △ around the pictures.
5. Short **u** words: Color the pictures.

Try This! Circle a short **i** word in this sentence.

Page 10

Name_____ Long vowels, Silent **e**

Silent E Words

Write the missing long vowel **a, i, o,** or **u** in the first blank. Write the silent **e** in the second blank.

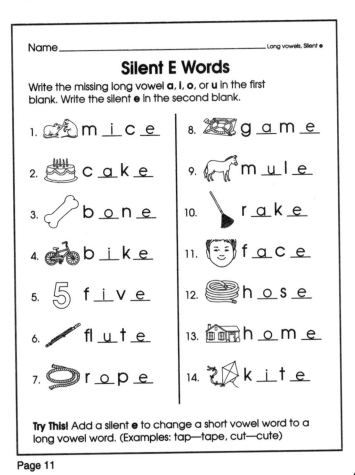

1. m i c e
2. c a k e
3. b o n e
4. b i k e
5. f i v e
6. fl u t e
7. r o p e

8. g a m e
9. m u l e
10. r a k e
11. f a c e
12. h o s e
13. h o m e
14. k i t e

Try This! Add a silent **e** to change a short vowel word to a long vowel word. (Examples: tap—tape, cut—cute)

Page 11

Name_____ Long vowels, Silent **e**

Long Vowels

Write the missing long vowel: **a, i, o,** or **u.**
Circle the silent **e.**

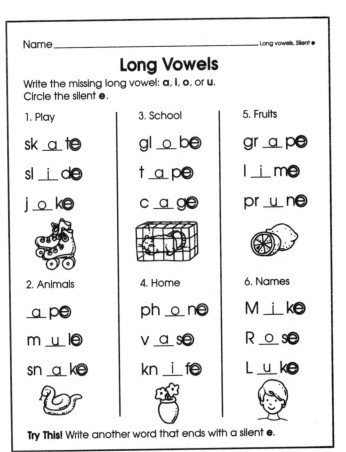

1. Play

sk a t e
sl i d e
j o k e

3. School

gl o b e
t a p e
c a g e

5. Fruits

gr a p e
l i m e
pr u n e

2. Animals

a p e
m u l e
sn a k e

4. Home

ph o n e
v a s e
kn i f e

6. Names

M i k e
R o s e
L u k e

Try This! Write another word that ends with a silent **e.**

Page 12

107

FS-32056 First Grade Review

Answer Key

It Takes Two

Match each word to its picture.
Underline the two vowels in each word.

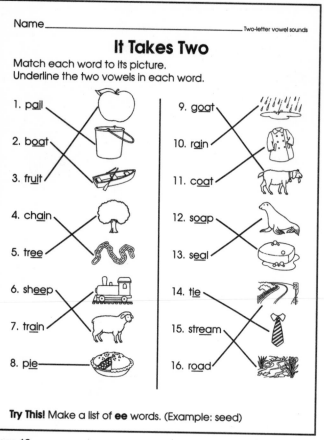

1. p<u>ai</u>l
2. b<u>oa</u>t
3. fr<u>ui</u>t
4. ch<u>ai</u>n
5. tr<u>ee</u>
6. sh<u>ee</u>p
7. tr<u>ai</u>n
8. p<u>ie</u>

9. g<u>oa</u>t
10. r<u>ai</u>n
11. c<u>oa</u>t
12. s<u>oa</u>p
13. s<u>ea</u>l
14. t<u>ie</u>
15. str<u>ea</u>m
16. r<u>oa</u>d

Try This! Make a list of **ee** words. (Example: seed)

Page 13

Y Can Be a Vowel

In the word *funny*, the **y** makes the long **e** sound.
In the word *dry*, the **y** makes the long **i** sound.
Say each word. Write it under the correct vowel sound.

baby   cry   fly   party

fry   story   city   sky

y sounds like e

baby

story

city

party

y sounds like i

fry

cry

fly

sky

Try This! Think of another word that ends with the letter **y**.
Does it sound like a long **e** or a long **i**?

Page 14

Rhyming Words

Circle the three pictures in each row that rhyme.

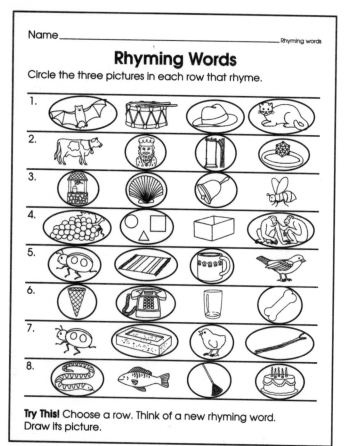

1.
2.
3.
4.
5.
6.
7.
8.

Try This! Choose a row. Think of a new rhyming word.
Draw its picture.

Page 15

Rhyme Time

Write the rhyming word that matches the picture.

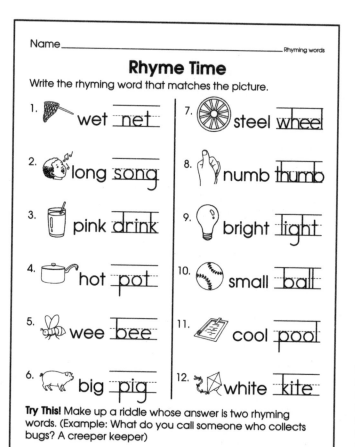

1. wet net
2. long song
3. pink drink
4. hot pot
5. wee bee
6. big pig

7. steel wheel
8. numb thumb
9. bright light
10. small ball
11. cool pool
12. white kite

Try This! Make up a riddle whose answer is two rhyming
words. (Example: What do you call someone who collects
bugs? A creeper keeper)

Page 16

Answer Key

Twins

Write the word from the fishtank that has the same meaning.

| large | begin | high | nice |
| earth | under | noisy | shut |

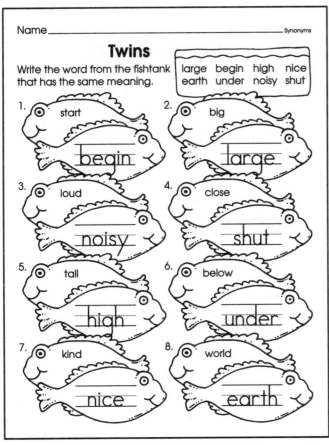

1. start — begin
2. big — large
3. loud — noisy
4. close — shut
5. tall — high
6. below — under
7. kind — nice
8. world — earth

Page 17

Working Animals

paths
road hard
find lift sea over

Write the word that means the same as the word in **dark** print.

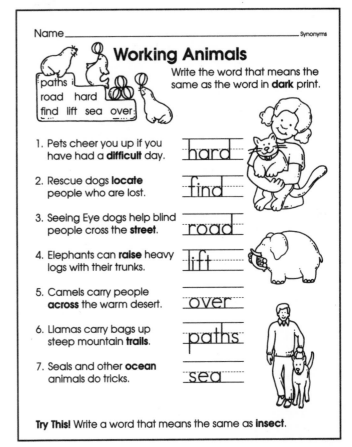

1. Pets cheer you up if you have had a **difficult** day. — hard
2. Rescue dogs **locate** people who are lost. — find
3. Seeing Eye dogs help blind people cross the **street**. — road
4. Elephants can **raise** heavy logs with their trunks. — lift
5. Camels carry people **across** the warm desert. — over
6. Llamas carry bags up steep mountain **trails**. — paths
7. Seals and other **ocean** animals do tricks. — sea

Try This! Write a word that means the same as **insect**.

Page 18

Up and Down

Match each word to its opposite.

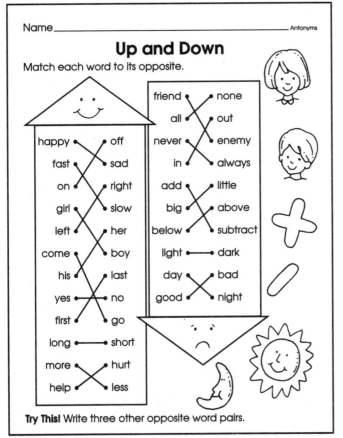

happy — sad
fast — slow
on — off
girl — boy
left — right
come — go
his — her
yes — no
first — last
long — short
more — less
help — hurt

friend — enemy
all — none
never — always
in — out
add — subtract
big — little
below — above
light — dark
day — night
good — bad

Try This! Write three other opposite word pairs.

Page 19

Your Amazing Body

Write the word that is the opposite of the word in **dark** print.

loud	left
cold	asleep
big	out

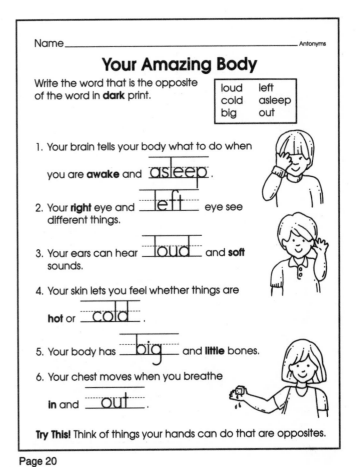

1. Your brain tells your body what to do when you are **awake** and asleep.
2. Your **right** eye and left eye see different things.
3. Your ears can hear loud and **soft** sounds.
4. Your skin lets you feel whether things are **hot** or cold.
5. Your body has big and **little** bones.
6. Your chest moves when you breathe **in** and out.

Try This! Think of things your hands can do that are opposites.

Page 20

FS-32056 First Grade Review

Answer Key

Animal Words

Name_____

Use a word from each wing to make one compound word for each picture.

dragon	star		frog	snake
blue	bull		dog	fly
grass	lady		bird	fish
sheep	rattle		bug	hopper

1. rattlesnake
2. grasshopper
3. sheepdog
4. dragonfly
5. ladybug
6. starfish
7. bullfrog
8. bluebird

Try This! See how many compound words you can think of in two minutes. Write them on the back of this paper.

Page 21

Jenny's Birthday

Name_____

Circle each compound word.
Write the compound word on the line.

1. It is Jenny's birthday.
   birthday
2. She jumps out of her daybed.
   daybed
3. She puts on a sweatshirt and jeans.
   sweatshirt
4. Next, Jenny helps make breakfast.
   breakfast
5. She eats a stack of pancakes.
   pancakes
6. Now Jenny can try out her new skateboard.
   skateboard
7. She runs outside and plays.
   outside

Try This! Write a list of things at home that are compound words.

Page 22

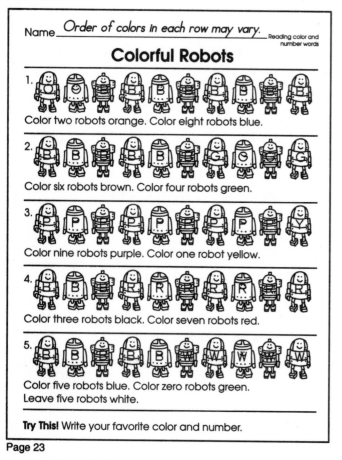

Name____ *Order of colors in each row may vary.*

Colorful Robots

1. Color two robots orange. Color eight robots blue.
2. Color six robots brown. Color four robots green.
3. Color nine robots purple. Color one robot yellow.
4. Color three robots black. Color seven robots red.
5. Color five robots blue. Color zero robots green.
   Leave five robots white.

Try This! Write your favorite color and number.

Page 23

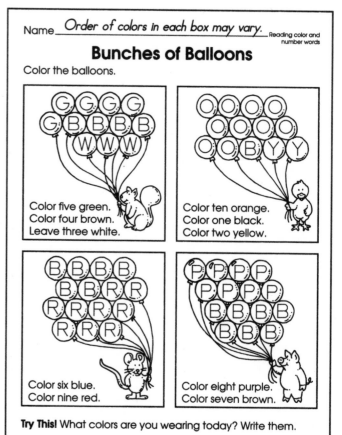

Name____ *Order of colors in each box may vary.*

Bunches of Balloons

Color the balloons.

Color five green.
Color four brown.
Leave three white.

Color ten orange.
Color one black.
Color two yellow.

Color six blue.
Color nine red.

Color eight purple.
Color seven brown.

Try This! What colors are you wearing today? Write them.

Page 24

FS-32056 First Grade Review

Answer Key

Find the Word

Fill in the circle next to the matching word.

1. ○ bug ● box ○ map
2. ○ house ○ sock ● hand
3. ○ purse ○ shoe ● plant
4. ○ rake ○ coat ● car
5. ○ brick ● boy ○ chair
6. ● dog ○ day ○ gum
7. ● drum ○ owl ○ door
8. ○ floor ● fire ○ spoon
9. ● road ○ train ○ ring
10. ○ comb ○ bike ● bus
11. ○ swim ○ gate ● star
12. ○ fall ● fish ○ yard
13. ● plane ○ park ○ nose
14. ● boat ○ hat ○ bring
15. ○ mad ● moon ○ jar
16. ● heart ○ zoo ○ him
17. ○ bird ○ queen ● ball
18. ○ knee ○ leaf ● cup

Try This! Draw pictures to match these words: **cat, rope, bug.**

Page 25

Which Picture?

Read the word. Circle the matching picture.

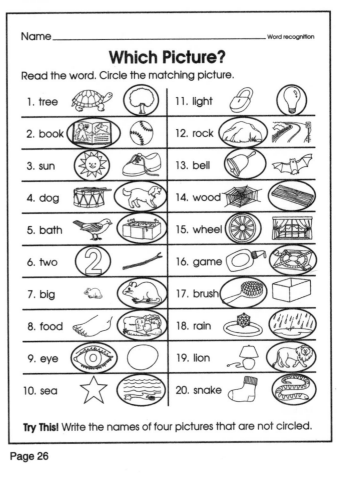

1. tree
2. book
3. sun
4. dog
5. bath
6. two
7. big
8. food
9. eye
10. sea
11. light
12. rock
13. bell
14. wood
15. wheel
16. game
17. brush
18. rain
19. lion
20. snake

Try This! Write the names of four pictures that are not circled.

Page 26

What Does It Say?

Circle the picture that matches each sentence.

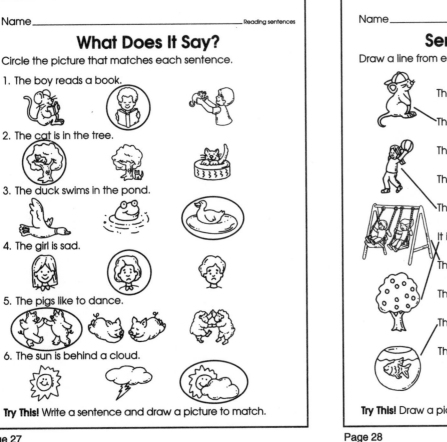

1. The boy reads a book.
2. The cat is in the tree.
3. The duck swims in the pond.
4. The girl is sad.
5. The pigs like to dance.
6. The sun is behind a cloud.

Try This! Write a sentence and draw a picture to match.

Page 27

Sentence Match-up

Draw a line from each sentence to its picture.

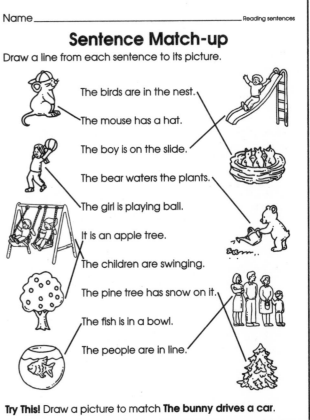

The birds are in the nest.
The mouse has a hat.
The boy is on the slide.
The bear waters the plants.
The girl is playing ball.
It is an apple tree.
The children are swinging.
The pine tree has snow on it.
The fish is in a bowl.
The people are in line.

Try This! Draw a picture to match **The bunny drives a car.**

Page 28

FS-32056 First Grade Review

Answer Key

Comprehension

Let's Go to School

Write the missing words.
Use words from the box.

walk	school
bus	late
car	ride

1. There are many ways to go to **school**.

2. Children who live nearby can **walk**.

3. If they are **late**, they need to run.

4. Some children ride the **bus**.

5. Others like to **ride** their bikes.

6. Parents can drive them in a **car**.

Try This! Draw a picture showing how you go to school.
Write a sentence to match.

Page 29

Name_____ Comprehension

All Kinds of Helpers

Write the missing words.
Use words from the box.

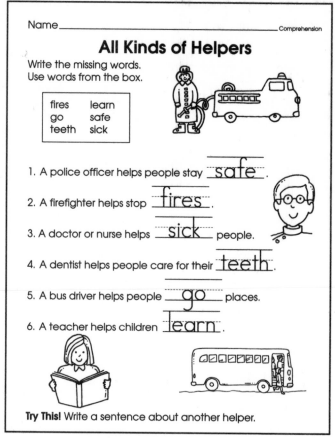

fires	learn
go	safe
teeth	sick

1. A police officer helps people stay **safe**.

2. A firefighter helps stop **fires**.

3. A doctor or nurse helps **sick** people.

4. A dentist helps people care for their **teeth**.

5. A bus driver helps people **go** places.

6. A teacher helps children **learn**.

Try This! Write a sentence about another helper.

Page 30

Name_____ Comprehension

A Nature Hike

Read the story. Write the answers.

Tina went on a hike.
She looked for leaves.
She listened to birds.
She smelled some flowers.
She felt a smooth rock.

1. Where did Tina go?
on a hike

2. What did she look for?
leaves

3. What did she hear?
birds

4. What did she touch?
a smooth rock

5. What did she use her nose for?
to smell some flowers

6. What would you do on a hike?
Answer varies.

Try This! Write something Tina might taste on a hike.

Page 31

Name_____ Comprehension

A Fun Trip

Read the story. Write the answers.

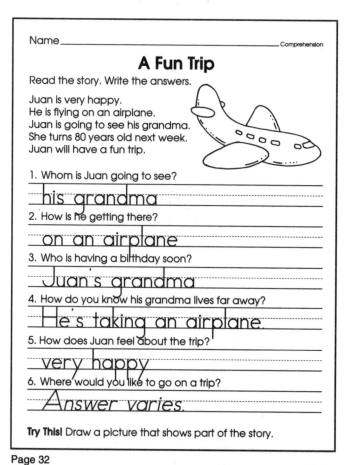

Juan is very happy.
He is flying on an airplane.
Juan is going to see his grandma.
She turns 80 years old next week.
Juan will have a fun trip.

1. Whom is Juan going to see?
his grandma

2. How is he getting there?
on an airplane

3. Who is having a birthday soon?
Juan's grandma

4. How do you know his grandma lives far away?
He's taking an airplane.

5. How does Juan feel about the trip?
very happy

6. Where would you like to go on a trip?
Answer varies.

Try This! Draw a picture that shows part of the story.

Page 32

112

Answer Key

Time for Dinner

Name_____ Main idea of a picture

Which sentence tells the main idea of the whole picture?
Fill in its circle.

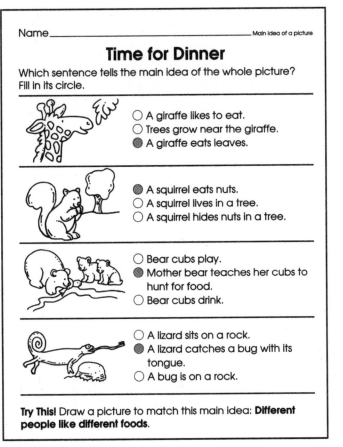

○ A giraffe likes to eat.
○ Trees grow near the giraffe.
● A giraffe eats leaves.

● A squirrel eats nuts.
○ A squirrel lives in a tree.
○ A squirrel hides nuts in a tree.

○ Bear cubs play.
● Mother bear teaches her cubs to hunt for food.
○ Bear cubs drink.

○ A lizard sits on a rock.
● A lizard catches a bug with its tongue.
○ A bug is on a rock.

Try This! Draw a picture to match this main idea: **Different people like different foods.**

Page 33

Summer Fun

Name_____ Main idea of a picture

Which sentence tells the main idea of the whole picture?
Fill in its circle.

● The children are selling lemonade.
○ The children made lemonade.
○ The children are outside.

○ Ken likes the pool.
● Ken likes swimming in the pool.
○ The pool is full of water.

○ Nan has a sister.
○ Nan is playing.
● Nan and her sister play together.

○ Brad is sleeping.
● Brad is picking flowers.
○ Flowers need to be watered.

Try This! Draw a picture showing what you like to do in the summer. Write a sentence about it.

Page 34

Family Time

Name_____ Main idea of a story

Fill in the circle of the sentence that tells the main idea of the story.

Tony likes to help his mom cook.
They make a lot of pasta.
Then they eat a lot of pasta.
Cooking with his mom is fun.

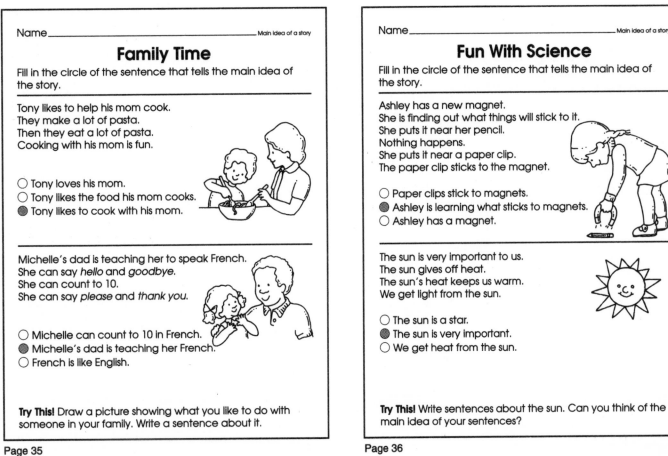

○ Tony loves his mom.
○ Tony likes the food his mom cooks.
● Tony likes to cook with his mom.

Michelle's dad is teaching her to speak French.
She can say *hello* and *goodbye*.
She can count to 10.
She can say *please* and *thank you*.

○ Michelle can count to 10 in French.
● Michelle's dad is teaching her French.
○ French is like English.

Try This! Draw a picture showing what you like to do with someone in your family. Write a sentence about it.

Page 35

Fun With Science

Name_____ Main idea of a story

Fill in the circle of the sentence that tells the main idea of the story.

Ashley has a new magnet.
She is finding out what things will stick to it.
She puts it near her pencil.
Nothing happens.
She puts it near a paper clip.
The paper clip sticks to the magnet.

○ Paper clips stick to magnets.
● Ashley is learning what sticks to magnets.
○ Ashley has a magnet.

The sun is very important to us.
The sun gives off heat.
The sun's heat keeps us warm.
We get light from the sun.

○ The sun is a star.
● The sun is very important.
○ We get heat from the sun.

Try This! Write sentences about the sun. Can you think of the main idea of your sentences?

Page 36

FS-32056 First Grade Review

Answer Key

Name _____ Reading a cover

What's on the Cover?

Look at the book's cover to answer the questions.

The **title** is the name of the book.

The **illustrator** is the person who drew the pictures.

The **author** is the person who wrote the book.

Tom's Turtle

By Emily Clark
Illustrations By Daniel Steele

What is the title of the book?

Tom's Turtle

Who is the author of the book?

Emily Clark

Who is the illustrator of the book?

Daniel Steele

Try This! Design your own book cover.

Page 37

Name ___ *Answers vary.* ___ Reading a cover

A New Cover

Read a book. Make a new cover for the book.
Write the title, the author, and the illustrator.
Draw a picture of your favorite part.

Title

Author

Illustrator

Try This! Look at the cover of two books. How are they alike and different?

Page 38

Name _____ Story parts—Beginning, middle, and end

Beginning, Middle, End

Read a story. Draw pictures that show what happened at the beginning, in the middle, and at the end.

Pictures and title will vary.

Beginning

Middle

End

Title

Page 39

Name ___ *Answers will vary.* ___ Story parts—Beginning, middle, and end

What Happened?

Read a book. Finish the sentences.

I read the book

At the beginning of the story

In the middle of the story

At the end of the story

Page 40

Answer Key

My Favorite Character

Think of your favorite book. Draw and label a picture of your favorite character from the book. Then finish the sentence.

Picture and answers will vary.

Character

_____

_____

I liked this character the best because _____

_____

_____

_____

_____

Try This! Write three ways you and the character are alike.

Page 41

An Important Character

Think of your favorite story. Draw the most important character from the story. Answer the questions.

Picture and answers will vary.

1. What is the character's name?

_____

2. What are three words that describe him or her?

_____

3. Why do you think this character is the most important?

_____

_____

Try This! If you were acting out the story, which character would you want to be? Write why.

Page 42

Reality or Fantasy?

Some stories are realistic. This means that the story could happen in real life.

Some stories are fantasy. This means the story could not happen in real life.

Read the sentences. Color the present red if it could really happen. Color the present green if it could not happen.

A dog is riding a bike. **G**

The rock is magic. **G**

Eggs come from a chicken. **R**

The cat played with the yarn. **R**

The pig put on his shirt. **G**

The bird built a nest. **R**

Nan went fishing. **R**

The boy rode in a plane. **R**

A fish went to the movies. **G**

The frog drives the bus. **G**

The girl can fly. **G**

The bear ate the fish. **R**

Try This! Draw a picture of a fantasy.

Page 43

Could It Really Happen?

Some stories are realistic. This means that the story could happen in real life.

Some stories are fantasy. This means the story could not happen in real life.

Read each sentence below. Color the scoop of ice cream blue if it could really happen. Color the scoop of ice cream yellow if it could not happen.

Ted sees a cloud. **B**

The spoon danced. **Y**

Bill threw the ball. **B**

Sue turned into a rock. **Y**

The sun ate lunch. **Y**

The boat is in the water. **B**

A turtle went skiing. **Y**

People run fast. **B**

A cow jumped over the moon. **Y**

The grass is blue. **Y**

Pam went to the zoo. **B**

Tom rode on a cloud. **Y**

Try This! Write three examples of things that could happen.

Page 44

© Frank Schaffer Publications, Inc.

115

FS-32056 First Grade Review

Answer Key

Name_____ _Alphabetical order—second letter_

At the Circus

Write each set of words in ABC order.

elephant   hat   tent

horse   tie   ticket

lion   wig   trapeze

balloon   children   peanuts

bear   circus   popcorn

bicycle   clown   program

Try This! Think of five funny clown names. Write them in ABC order.

Page 45

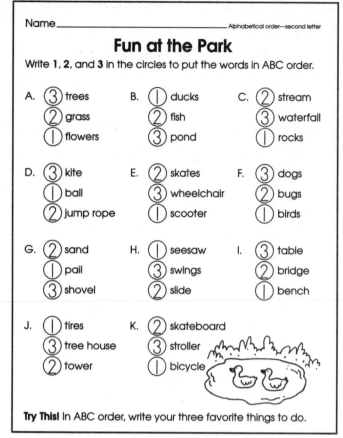

Name_____ _Alphabetical order—second letter_

Fun at the Park

Write **1**, **2**, and **3** in the circles to put the words in ABC order.

A. ③ trees   B. ① ducks   C. ② stream
    ② grass   ② fish   ③ waterfall
    ① flowers   ③ pond   ① rocks

D. ③ kite   E. ② skates   F. ③ dogs
    ① ball   ③ wheelchair   ② bugs
    ② jump rope   ① scooter   ① birds

G. ② sand   H. ① seesaw   I. ③ table
    ① pail   ③ swings   ② bridge
    ③ shovel   ② slide   ① bench

J. ① tires   K. ② skateboard
    ③ tree house   ③ stroller
    ② tower   ① bicycle

Try This! In ABC order, write your three favorite things to do.

Page 46

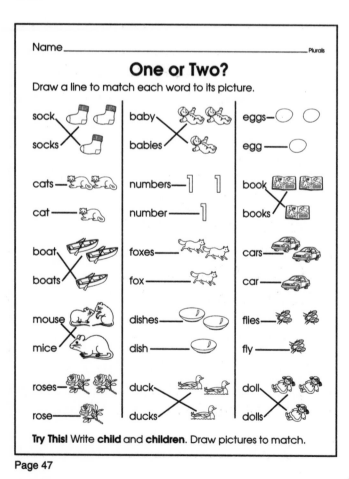

Name_____ _Plurals_

One or Two?

Draw a line to match each word to its picture.

sock / socks   baby / babies   eggs / egg

cats / cat   numbers / number   book / books

boat / boats   foxes / fox   cars / car

mouse / mice   dishes / dish   flies / fly

roses / rose   duck / ducks   doll / dolls

Try This! Write **child** and **children**. Draw pictures to match.

Page 47

Name_____ _Plurals_

More Than One

Write the missing words that match the pictures.

1. hand   hands
2. ball   balls
3. box   boxes
4. star   stars
5. tree   trees
6. home   homes
7. eye   eyes
8. bird   birds

Try This! Fill in the blanks with numbers. Then draw the monster.
The monster has ___ eyes, ___ mouths, ___ arms, and ___ legs.

Page 48

Answer Key

Name_____ Capitalizing names

Names, Names, Names
Write the names. Begin each with a capital letter.

james — James

mrs. yee — Mrs. Yee

kyle — Kyle

mr. larson — Mr. Larson

anna — Anna

sarah — Sarah

nicole — Nicole

joseph — Joseph

ms. lopez — Ms. Lopez

marco — Marco

miss ray — Miss Ray

ian — Ian

Try This! Write your full name on the back of this paper.

Page 49

Name_____ *Answers will vary.* Capitalizing names

You Pick the Name
Write a name in the blank. Begin each with a capital letter.

1. _____ wants to be an astronaut.

2. _____ likes animals.

3. _____ is a very smart dog.

4. _____ and _____ are friends.

5. Mrs. _____ works at our school.

6. _____ is good at art.

7. I know someone named Mr. _____ .

8. My last name is _____ ,

9. _____ likes to ride her bike.

10. _____ can sing really well.

Try This! Write your favorite name.

Page 50

Name_____ Capitalization, Syntax

All Mixed-up!
Write the words in the correct order to make sentences. The first word in a sentence begins with a capital letter.

1. are   big.   Whales
   Whales are big.

2. sea.   They   in   the   live
   They live in the sea.

3. They   swim.   can
   They can swim.

4. not   are   fish.   Whales
   Whales are not fish.

5. mammals.   They   are
   They are mammals.

6. drink   whales   milk.   Baby
   Baby whales drink milk.

Try This! Write your own sentence about whales.

Page 51

Name_____ Capitalization, Syntax

Kim's Kitten
Write the words in the correct order to make sentences. The first word in a sentence begins with a capital letter.

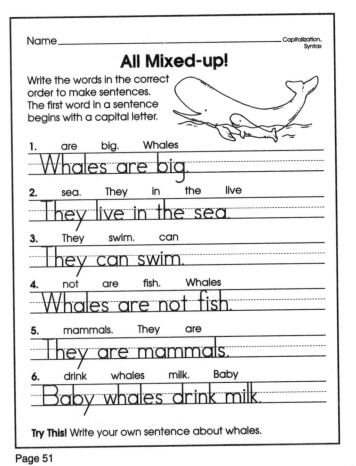

1. girl.   Kim   a   is
   Kim is a girl.

2. very   is   She   smart.
   She is very smart.

3. wanted   Kim   pet.   a
   Kim wanted a pet.

4. She   kitten.   a   got
   She got a kitten.

5. kitten.   loved   her   Kim
   Kim loved her kitten.

6. with   played   her   Kim   kitten.
   Kim played with her kitten.

Try This! What pet would you like? Write a sentence about it.

Page 52

FS-32056 First Grade Review

Answer Key

Name_____

Period, Question mark

A Trip to the Zoo

Read each sentence.
Circle the • if it is a telling sentence.
Circle the ? if it is an asking sentence.

1. We went to the zoo   (•)   ?
2. Have you been to a zoo   •   (?)
3. We saw lots of animals   (•)   ?
4. The elephants were big   (•)   ?
5. Next, we saw the giraffes   (•)   ?
6. Are you as tall as a giraffe   •   (?)
7. The monkeys were funny   (•)   ?
8. They chase each other   (•)   ?
9. Do you like to play chase   •   (?)
10. What is your favorite animal   •   (?)
11. We liked the sea lions the best   (•)   ?
12. They played in the water   (•)   ?

Try This! Write a telling sentence and an asking sentence about the zoo. Make sure to put a period (•) or a question mark (?) at the end.

Page 53

Name_____

Period, Question mark

Planting a Garden

Read each sentence.
Write a • at the end if it is a telling sentence.
Write a ? at the end if it is an asking sentence.

1. We are planting a garden.
2. Have you ever had a garden?
3. First, we need to pull up the weeds.
4. Then we will make the soil loose.
5. Have you ever seen a worm?
6. There are lots of worms in the soil.
7. Next, we will plant the seeds.
8. What is your favorite vegetable?
9. We are planting beans and carrots.
10. We will also grow corn and peppers.
11. Our garden needs sunshine and water.
12. Would you like to plant a garden?

Try This! Write an asking sentence about a garden. Give it to a partner to answer.

Page 54

Name_____ *Spelling words will vary.*

Spelling

Spelling Practice

Choose words you need to practice.
Write each word twice on the matching dogs.

Try This! Trace each word with a crayon.

Page 55

Name_____ *Spelling words will vary.*

Spelling

Make a Spelling Puzzle

Choose spelling words you need to practice.
Write them in the empty puzzle.
Fill the extra boxes with letters.
Now look for your words and color them.
Write the words you found on the lines.

Try This! Read each word. Then close your eyes and spell it aloud. Open your eyes and check. Did you spell it right?

Page 56

118

Answer Key

Name

Answers will vary.

Plan a Story

1. What kind of story do you want to write?
   Fill in all the circles that answer the question:
   - ○ true
   - ○ make-believe that could really happen
   - ○ make-believe that couldn't really happen
   - ○ funny
   - ○ serious
   - ○ scary
   - ○ other _____

2. What kind of characters will you have?
   Fill in all the circles that answer the question:
   - ○ people I know
   - ○ people I make up
   - ○ animals I know
   - ○ animals I make up
   - ○ make-believe creatures

   Write the names of your characters.

Try This! Where will your story take place? Draw it on the back.

Page 57

Name

Answers will vary.

Story Ideas

What do you want to happen in your story?
Write three ideas.
Draw a star by your favorite one.

1.

2.

3.

What would be
a good title for
your story?

Try This! Meet with a partner. Read and listen to each other's ideas. Ask your partner which idea he or she likes best.

Page 58

Name

My Trip

Think of a trip that you went on. Draw a picture of your favorite part of the trip. Then write a sentence describing it.

Picture and sentence will vary.

Try This! Write where you would like to go on a trip.

Page 59

Name

Think Back

What is your favorite thing to do at school?
Draw a picture of it. Then write about it.

Picture and writing will vary.

Try This! Read what you wrote. Did you leave out any words?

Page 60

Answer Key

Questions will vary.

Name_____ Writing questions

Friendly Questions

Meet with a partner.
Think of questions to ask each other.
Write the questions. Then trade papers. Write your answers.

Question _____
_____
_____
_____

Answer _____
_____
_____

Question _____
_____
_____

Answer _____
_____
_____

Try This! Which do you like better—asking or answering? Why?

Page 61

Questions will vary.

Name_____ Writing questions

Nice to Meet You

Yikes! A talking dinosaur just
entered your classroom.
Write two questions you will ask it.
Then write its answers.

Question _____
_____
_____
_____

Answer _____
_____

Question _____
_____
_____

Answer _____
_____

Try This! Write a question the dinosaur might ask you.

Page 62

Name_____ Writing an invitation

A Tasty Tea Party

The Big Bad Wolf is having a tea party.
He's hoping to eat any little pigs that show up!
The party will be held in the deep, dark forest.
It will be on Friday, May 5, at 10 o'clock.

Write the invitation.

Please come
to my tea
party!

Date Friday, May 5

Time 10 o'clock

Place Deep, dark forest

Given by Big Bad Wolf

Try This! Pretend you are a pig. Send your reply to the wolf.

Page 63

Name_____ Writing an invitation

Come to My Party!

Pretend you are having a party at your house.
It can be any kind of party you want.
Write the invitation.
Draw pictures to decorate it.

Pictures and answers will vary.

What _____

Date _____

Time _____

Place _____

Given by _____

Try This! Make a list of the things you would need to do to get ready for your party.

Page 64

Answer Key

Name_____

Notes will vary.

Writing a thank-you note

Folk Tale Thank-you Note

Choose a folk tale you know. Think of how one character helped another. Example:

The woodcutter saved Little Red Riding Hood.

Pretend you are the character who was helped. Write a thank-you note to the other character.

Thank you!

Try This! Whom could you make a thank-you note for? Write the person's name and what you would thank him or her for.

Page 65

Name_____

Notes will vary.

Writing a thank-you note

Thank You!

Think of someone who has helped you lately.
Write him or her a thank-you note.

Thank you!

Try This! Cut out your note. Glue it to a piece of colored paper. Trim the edges. Give it to your helper.

Page 66

Student colors in pencils after each step is completed.

Name_____

Revising and proofreading

Check Your Writing

Write a story. Work with a partner.
Color the pencil after you do each step.

1 Read aloud what you wrote.
Listen for these things:
- missing words
- extra words
- parts that don't make sense

2 Read aloud what you wrote.
Look for these things:
- a capital letter at the beginning of each sentence
- a punctuation mark (. or ? or !) at the end of each sentence

3 Read aloud what you wrote.
Look for this:
- words that are spelled wrong

~~knit~~ *knight*

Partner's name _____

Try This! Would you rather work alone or with a partner? Why?

Page 67

Name_____

Revising and proofreading

X Marks the Spot

Write a story. Do this page when you finish writing.
Mark an **X** in the **Yes** or **No** column as you answer each question.
Fix the parts that need it.

Answers will vary.

Yes	No	
		Are there any missing words or extra words?
		Do all sentences make sense?
		Do you want to add anything else?
		Do all names and sentences begin with a capital letter?
		Do all sentences end with a punctuation mark (. or ! or ?)?
		Are there any words you need help spelling?

Try This! Are any words too sloppy to read? If yes, fix them.

Page 68

Answer Key

Name _Answers vary. Accept reasonable answers._ Classifying

That Doesn't Belong!

Cross out the word that doesn't belong.
Write a new word for each group.

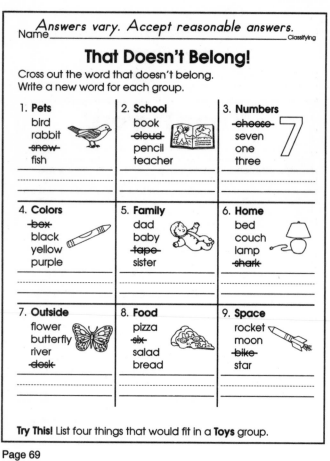

1. **Pets**
   bird
   rabbit
   ~~snow~~
   fish

2. **School**
   book
   ~~cloud~~
   pencil
   teacher

3. **Numbers**
   ~~choose~~
   seven
   one
   three
   7

4. **Colors**
   ~~box~~
   black
   yellow
   purple

5. **Family**
   dad
   baby
   ~~tape~~
   sister

6. **Home**
   bed
   couch
   lamp
   ~~shark~~

7. **Outside**
   flower
   butterfly
   river
   ~~desk~~

8. **Food**
   pizza
   ~~six~~
   salad
   bread

9. **Space**
   rocket
   moon
   ~~bike~~
   star

Try This! List four things that would fit in a **Toys** group.

Page 69

Name _Accept reasonable answers._ Classifying

Name the Group

Write a title that names each group of pictures.

1. shapes
2. birds
3. tools
4. fish
5. fruit
6. flowers
7. clothes
8. bugs

Try This! Draw another picture for each row.

Page 70

Name _Answers vary. Accept reasonable answers._ Analyzing

Alike and Different

How are a globe and a ball alike?

How are they different?

How are you and a pencil alike?

How are you different?

Try This! Name something else that is like you and the pencil.

Page 71

Name _Answers vary. Accept reasonable answers._ Analyzing

At the Farm

Use words from the picture for the first two blanks.
Then finish each sentence.

tree barn
house
chick hen sheep cow horse duck pig pond

1. A _____ is like a _____ because

2. A _____ is like a _____ because

3. A _____ is like a _____ because

Try This! Who in your family is most like you? Why?

Page 72

FS-32056 First Grade Review

Answer Key

Watch Us Grow

Draw the missing pictures.
Number the boxes 1, 2, and 3 to show the order.

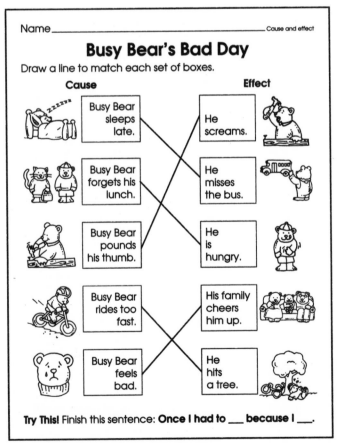

Try This! Work with a friend. Draw how a butterfly grows.

Page 73

First, Next, Then, Last

Number the boxes 1, 2, 3, and 4 to show the order.

Try This! How do you go to bed? Draw and number the steps.

Page 74

Busy Bear's Bad Day

Draw a line to match each set of boxes.

Cause   **Effect**

Cause	Effect
Busy Bear sleeps late.	He screams.
Busy Bear forgets his lunch.	He misses the bus.
Busy Bear pounds his thumb.	He is hungry.
Busy Bear rides too fast.	His family cheers him up.
Busy Bear feels bad.	He hits a tree.

Try This! Finish this sentence: **Once I had to ___ because I ___.**

Page 75

What Might Happen?

Draw a picture that shows what might happen.

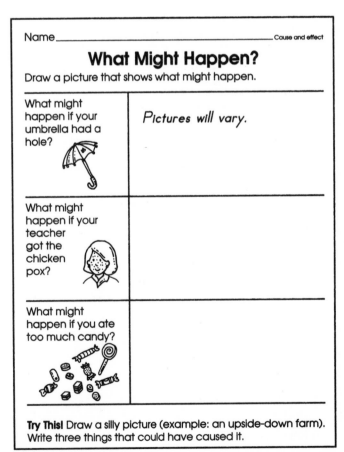

What might happen if your umbrella had a hole?	*Pictures will vary.*
What might happen if your teacher got the chicken pox?	
What might happen if you ate too much candy?	

Try This! Draw a silly picture (example: an upside-down farm). Write three things that could have caused it.

Page 76

Answer Key

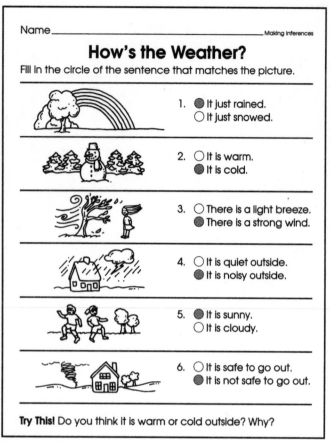

Name_____ Making Inferences

How's the Weather?

Fill in the circle of the sentence that matches the picture.

1. ● It just rained.
   ○ It just snowed.

2. ○ It is warm.
   ● It is cold.

3. ○ There is a light breeze.
   ● There is a strong wind.

4. ○ It is quiet outside.
   ● It is noisy outside.

5. ● It is sunny.
   ○ It is cloudy.

6. ○ It is safe to go out.
   ● It is not safe to go out.

Try This! Do you think it is warm or cold outside? Why?

Page 77

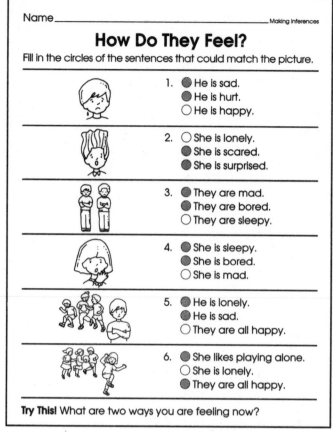

Name_____ Making Inferences

How Do They Feel?

Fill in the circles of the sentences that could match the picture.

1. ● He is sad.
   ● He is hurt.
   ○ He is happy.

2. ○ She is lonely.
   ● She is scared.
   ● She is surprised.

3. ● They are mad.
   ● They are bored.
   ○ They are sleepy.

4. ● She is sleepy.
   ● She is bored.
   ○ She is mad.

5. ● He is lonely.
   ● He is sad.
   ○ They are all happy.

6. ● She likes playing alone.
   ○ She is lonely.
   ● They are all happy.

Try This! What are two ways you are feeling now?

Page 78

Name *Answers vary. Accept reasonable answers.*
_____ Evaluating

Sea Life

Use words from the picture for the first two blanks.
Then finish each sentence.

crab   sea gull   whale   pelican
dolphin
starfish   shark
sea horse   squid

1. I would rather **meet** a _____ than a

   _____ because _____

2. I would rather **be** a _____ than a

   _____ because _____

Try This! What is your favorite sea animal? Why?

Page 79

Name *Answers vary. Accept reasonable answers.*
_____ Evaluating

A Long Time Ago

Use words from the picture for the first two blanks.
Then finish each sentence.

castle   forest
princess
horse   knight   dragon   cave

1. I would rather **meet** a _____ than a

   _____ because _____

2. I would rather **be** a _____ than a

   _____ because _____

Try This! Would you rather live now or in the time of castles?
Write why.

Page 80

FS-32056 First Grade Review

Answer Key

Page 83 — Liftoff!

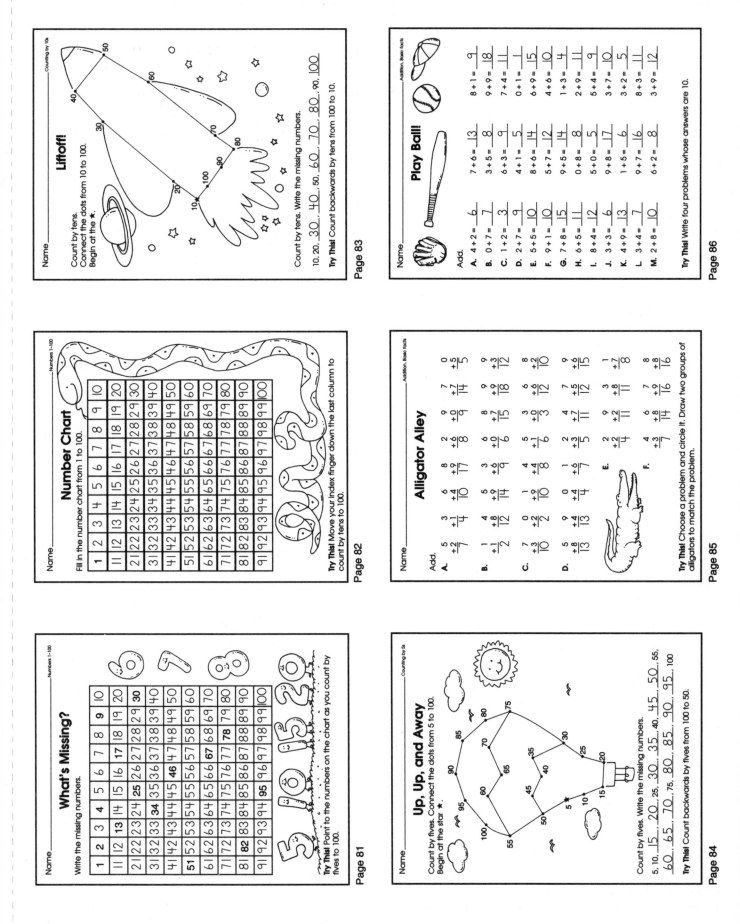

Count by tens.
Connect the dots from 10 to 100.
Begin at the ★.

Count by tens. Write the missing numbers.
10, 20, 30, 40, 50, 60, 70, 80, 90, 100

Try This! Count backwards by tens from 100 to 10.

Page 83

Page 82 — Number Chart

Numbers 1–100

Fill in the number chart from 1 to 100.

1	2	3	4	5	6	7	8	9	10
11	12	13	14	15	16	17	18	19	20
21	22	23	24	25	26	27	28	29	30
31	32	33	34	35	36	37	38	39	40
41	42	43	44	45	46	47	48	49	50
51	52	53	54	55	56	57	58	59	60
61	62	63	64	65	66	67	68	69	70
71	72	73	74	75	76	77	78	79	80
81	82	83	84	85	86	87	88	89	90
91	92	93	94	95	96	97	98	99	100

Try This! Move your index finger down the last column to count by tens to 100.

Page 82

Page 81 — What's Missing?

Numbers 1–100

Write the missing numbers.

1	2	3	4	5	6	7	8	9	10
11	12	**13**	14	15	16	**17**	18	19	20
21	22	23	24	**25**	26	27	28	29	**30**
31	32	33	**34**	35	36	37	38	39	40
41	42	43	44	45	**46**	47	48	49	50
51	52	53	54	55	56	57	58	59	60
61	62	63	64	65	66	**67**	68	69	70
71	72	73	74	75	76	77	**78**	79	80
81	**82**	83	84	85	86	87	88	89	90
91	92	93	94	**95**	96	97	98	99	100

5, 10, 15, 20, 25...

Try This! Point to the numbers on the chart as you count by fives to 100.

Page 81

Page 86 — Play Ball!

Addition, Basic facts

Add.

A. $4+2=6$	$7+6=13$	$8+1=9$
B. $0+7=7$	$3+5=8$	$9+9=18$
C. $1+2=3$	$6+3=9$	$7+4=11$
D. $2+7=9$	$4+1=5$	$0+1=1$
E. $5+5=10$	$8+6=14$	$6+9=15$
F. $9+1=10$	$5+7=12$	$4+6=10$
G. $7+8=15$	$9+5=14$	$1+3=4$
H. $6+5=11$	$0+8=8$	$2+9=11$
I. $8+4=12$	$5+0=5$	$5+4=9$
J. $3+3=6$	$9+8=17$	$3+7=10$
K. $4+9=13$	$1+5=6$	$3+2=5$
L. $3+4=7$	$9+7=16$	$1+1=2$
M. $2+8=10$	$6+2=8$	$3+9=12$

Try This! Write four problems whose answers are 10.

Page 86

Page 85 — Alligator Alley

Addition, Basic facts

Add.

A.	$5+2=7$	$3+1=4$	$6+4=10$	$8+9=17$	$2+6=8$	$9+0=9$	$7+7=14$	$0+5=5$
B.	$1+1=2$	$4+8=12$	$5+9=14$	$3+6=9$	$6+0=6$	$8+7=15$	$9+9=18$	$9+3=12$
C.	$7+3=10$	$0+2=2$	$1+9=10$	$4+4=8$	$5+1=6$	$3+0=3$	$6+6=12$	$8+2=10$
D.	$5+8=13$	$9+4=13$	$0+4=4$	$1+6=7$	$2+3=5$	$4+7=11$	$7+5=12$	$9+6=15$
E.	$2+2=4$	$3+8=11$	$1+7=8$					
F.	$4+3=7$	$6+8=14$	$9+7=16$	$8+8=16$				

Try This! Choose a problem and circle it. Draw two groups of alligators to match the problem.

Page 85

Page 84 — Up, Up, and Away

Counting by 5s

Count by fives. Connect the dots from 5 to 100.
Begin at the star ★.

Count by fives. Write the missing numbers.
5, 10, 15, 20, 25, 30, 35, 40, 45, 50, 55, 100

Try This! Count backwards by fives from 100 to 50.
60, 65, 70, 75, 80, 85, 90, 95, 100

Page 84

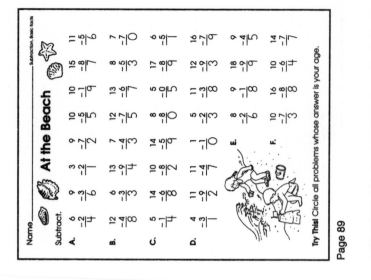
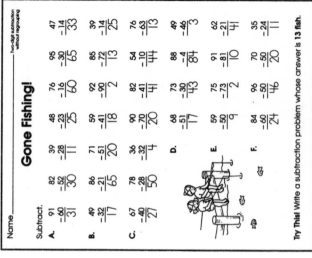

At the Beach — Subtraction, Basic facts

Name _____

Subtract.

Try This! Circle all problems whose answer is your age.

Page 89

Gone Fishing! — Two-digit subtraction without regrouping

Name _____

Subtract.

Try This! Write a subtraction problem whose answer is **13 fish.**

Page 92

Elephant Parade — Two-digit addition

Name _____

Add.

Try This! Make up a problem whose answer is **20 elephants.**

Page 88

Spring Flowers — Two-digit subtraction without regrouping

Name _____

Subtract.

Try This! Check your work by adding your answer to the number subtracted. (Example: 83 − 63 = 20; 20 + 63 = 83)

Page 91

Rainy Day — Two-digit addition

Name _____

Add.

Try This! Do these in your head: **60 + 30 = 90   22 + 55 = 77**

Page 87

Shining Stars — Subtraction, Basic facts

Name _____

Subtract.

A. 7 − 3 = 4
B. 8 − 7 = 1
C. 4 − 2 = 2
D. 7 − 6 = 1
E. 5 − 3 = 2
F. 4 − 4 = 0
G. 3 − 0 = 3
H. 6 − 1 = 5
I. 8 − 4 = 4
J. 2 − 2 = 0
K. 9 − 6 = 3
L. 2 − 1 = 1
M. 7 − 2 = 5

14 − 8 = 6
11 − 8 = 3
15 − 6 = 9
13 − 4 = 9
17 − 8 = 9
13 − 8 = 5
10 − 9 = 1
12 − 3 = 9
18 − 9 = 9
15 − 7 = 8
14 − 9 = 5
12 − 8 = 4
14 − 7 = 7

16 − 9 = 7
11 − 2 = 9
12 − 5 = 7
11 − 7 = 4
10 − 2 = 8
12 − 6 = 6
10 − 3 = 7
17 − 9 = 8
10 − 4 = 6
16 − 8 = 8
10 − 5 = 5
11 − 6 = 5
13 − 7 = 6

Try This! Write two subtraction problems using **5, 7, and 12.**

Page 90

FS-32056 First Grade Review

Answer Key

Number Patterns

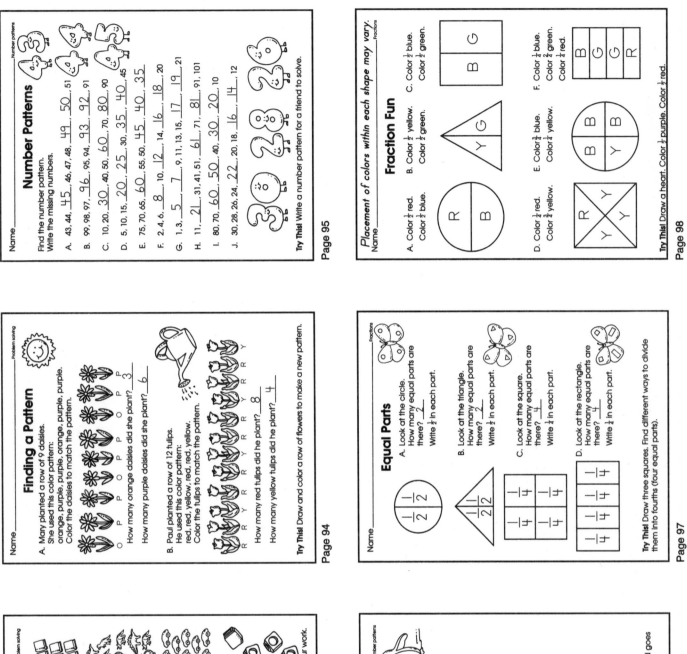

Find the number pattern.
Write the missing numbers.

A. 43, 44, _45_, 46, 47, 48, _49_, _50_, _51_

B. 99, 98, 97, _96_, 95, 94, _93_, _92_, _91_

C. 10, 20, _30_, 40, 50, _60_, 70, _80_, _90_

D. 5, 10, 15, _20_, _25_, 30, _35_, 40, _45_

E. 75, 70, 65, _60_, 55, 50, _45_, _40_, _35_

F. 2, 4, 6, _8_, 10, _12_, 14, _16_, _18_, _20_

G. 1, 3, _5_, _7_, 9, 11, 13, 15, _17_, _19_, _21_

H. 11, _21_, 31, 41, 51, _61_, 71, _81_, _91_, 101

I. 80, 70, _60_, _50_, 40, _30_, _20_, 10

J. 30, 28, 26, 24, _22_, 20, 18, _16_, _14_, 12

Try This! Write a number pattern for a friend to solve.

Page 95

Placement of colors within each shape may vary.

Fraction Fun

A. Color ½ red.
Color ½ blue.

B. Color ½ yellow.
Color ½ green.

C. Color ½ blue.
Color ½ green.

D. Color ¼ red.
Color ¾ yellow.

E. Color ⅓ blue.
Color ⅓ yellow.

F. Color ¼ blue.
Color ½ green.
Color ¼ red.

Try This! Draw a heart. Color ½ purple. Color ½ red.

Page 98

Finding a Pattern

A. Mary planted a row of 9 daisies.
She used this color pattern:
orange, purple, purple, orange, purple, purple.
Color the daisies to match the pattern.

How many orange daisies did she plant? _3_

How many purple daisies did she plant? _6_

B. Paul planted a row of 12 tulips.
He used this color pattern:
red, red, yellow, red, red, yellow.
Color the tulips to match the pattern.

How many red tulips did he plant? _8_

How many yellow tulips did he plant? _4_

Try This! Draw and color a row of flowers to make a new pattern.

Page 94

Equal Parts

A. Look at the circle.
How many equal parts are
there? _2_
Write ½ in each part.

B. Look at the triangle.
How many equal parts are
there? _2_
Write ½ in each part.

C. Look at the square.
How many equal parts does
there? _4_
Write ¼ in each part.

D. Look at the rectangle.
How many equal parts are
there? _4_
Write ¼ in each part.

Try This! Draw three squares. Find different ways to divide them into fourths (four equal parts).

Page 97

Guess and Check

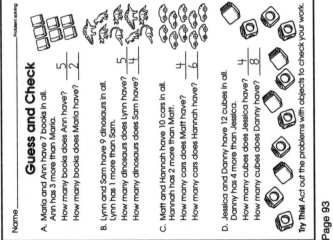

A. Maria and Ann have 7 books in all.
Ann has 3 more than Maria.
How many books does Ann have? _5_
How many books does Maria have? _2_

B. Lynn and Sam have 9 dinosaurs in all.
Lynn has 1 more than Sam.
How many dinosaurs does Lynn have? _5_
How many dinosaurs does Sam have? _4_

C. Matt and Hannah have 10 cars in all.
Hannah has 2 more than Matt.
How many cars does Matt have? _4_
How many cars does Hannah have? _6_

D. Jessica and Danny have 12 cubes in all.
Danny has 4 more than Jessica.
How many cubes does Jessica have? _4_
How many cubes does Danny have? _8_

Try This! Act out the problems with objects to check your work.

Page 93

What Comes Next?

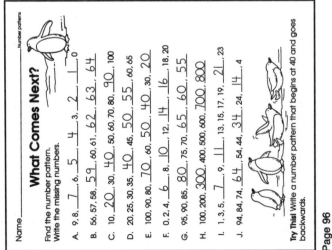

Find the number pattern.
Write the missing numbers.

A. 9, 8, _7_, 6, _5_, 4, _3_, 2, _1_, 0

B. 56, 57, 58, _59_, 60, 61, _62_, 63, _64_

C. 10, _20_, 30, _40_, 50, 60, 70, 80, _90_, 100

D. 20, 25, 30, 35, _40_, 45, _50_, 55, 60, 65

E. 100, 90, 80, _70_, 60, _50_, 40, 30, _20_

F. 0, 2, 4, _6_, _8_, 10, _12_, 14, 16, 18, 20

G. 95, 90, 85, _80_, 75, 70, _65_, 60, 55

H. 100, 200, _300_, 400, 500, 600, _700_, _800_

I. 1, 3, 5, _7_, 9, _11_, 13, 15, 17, 19, _21_, 23

J. 94, 84, 74, _64_, 54, 44, _34_, 24, _14_, 4

Try This! Write a number pattern that begins at 40 and goes backwards.

Page 96

Answer Key

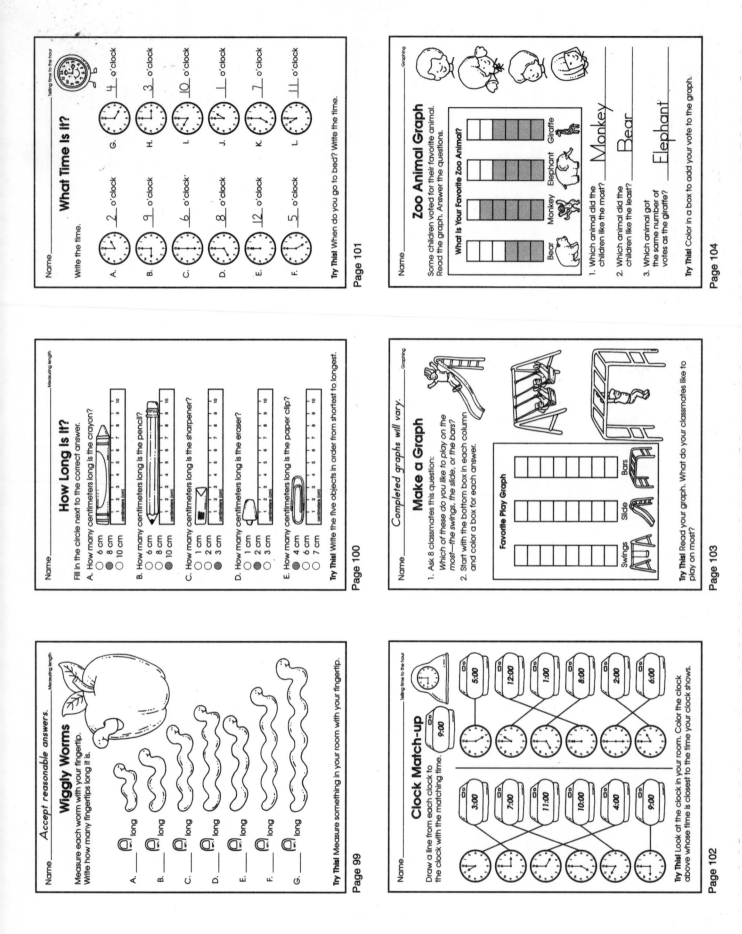

Page 99

Name _____

Accept reasonable answers.

Wiggly Worms

Measure each worm with your fingertip.
Write how many fingertips long it is.

A. ___ ⌣ long
B. ___ ⌣ long
C. ___ ⌣ long
D. ___ ⌣ long
E. ___ ⌣ long
F. ___ ⌣ long
G. ___ ⌣ long

Try This! Measure something in your room with your fingertip.

Page 100

Name _____   Measuring length

How Long Is It?

Fill in the circle next to the correct answer.

A. How many centimeters long is the crayon?
○ 6 cm
○ 8 cm
● 10 cm

B. How many centimeters long is the pencil?
○ 6 cm
○ 8 cm
● 10 cm

C. How many centimeters long is the sharpener?
○ 1 cm
○ 2 cm
● 3 cm

D. How many centimeters long is the eraser?
○ 1 cm
● 2 cm
○ 3 cm

E. How many centimeters long is the paper clip?
● 4 cm
○ 6 cm
○ 7 cm

Try This! Write the five objects in order from shortest to longest.

Page 101

Name _____   Telling time to the hour

What Time Is It?

Write the time.

A. 2 o'clock
B. 9 o'clock
C. 6 o'clock
D. 8 o'clock
E. 12 o'clock
F. 5 o'clock

G. 4 o'clock
H. 3 o'clock
I. 10 o'clock
J. 1 o'clock
K. 7 o'clock
L. 11 o'clock

Try This! When do you go to bed? Write the time.

Page 102

Name _____   Telling time to the hour

Clock Match-up

Draw a line from each clock to the clock with the matching time.

3:00 7:00 11:00 10:00 4:00 9:00

5:00 12:00 1:00 8:00 2:00 6:00

Try This! Look at the clock in your room. Color the clock above whose time is closest to the time your clock shows.

Page 103

Name _____   Graphing

Completed graphs will vary.

Make a Graph

1. Ask 8 classmates this question:
   Which of these do you like to play on the most—the swings, the slide, or the bars?
2. Start with the bottom box in each column and color a box for each answer.

Favorite Play Graph

Swings   Slide   Bars

Try This! Read your graph. What do your classmates like to play on most?

Page 104

Name _____   Graphing

Zoo Animal Graph

Some children voted for their favorite animal.
Read the graph. Answer the questions.

What Is Your Favorite Zoo Animal?

Bear   Monkey   Elephant   Giraffe

1. Which animal did the children like the most?   Monkey

2. Which animal did the children like the least?   Bear

3. Which animal got the same number of votes as the giraffe?   Elephant

Try This! Color in a box to add your vote to the graph.

128